Social Media Marketing

Step-by-Step Strategies for Marketing and Advertising Your Business to Millions on Facebook, Instagram, YouTube and Twitter, While Branding Yourself or Your Business as an Influencer in 2019 and Beyond

By

Gary Clyne

Table of Contents

Introduction_____ 5

The Importance of Social Media _____ 7

Statistics Don't Lie _____ 8

Why My Business Needs Social Media? ____10

Web Traffic _____ 11

Connecting with Customers _____13

Improving Your Brand's Image _____15

Getting Started With Social Media Marketing17

Making Your Social Media Marketing Plan 17

The Best 5 Social Media Marketing
Strategies to Increase Productivity _____ 22

Killer Content is the Key _____ 26

Facebook _____ 29

Creating Your Facebook Page_____ 30

Getting Your Fans _____ 36

Posting Like a Pro _____ 38

Optimizing for SEO _____ 43

The Right Marketing Strategy _____47

Tracking Your Results_____53

Advertising on Facebook _____55

YouTube _____ 65

   Creating Your Business Profile _____ 65

   Optimizing for SEO _____ 70

   Making the Videos _____77

   Marketing the Videos _____ 86

   Getting a Handle on YouTube Analytics___ 91

   Advertising on YouTube _____ 94

Instagram _____100

   Setting Up Your Instagram Business
   Account _____100

   Types of Insta Posts _____ 105

   Writing Eye-Catching Captions _____ 114

   Marketing Your Brand _____ 118

   Attracting Followers _____ 122

   What About Analytics? _____ 126

   Advertising on Instagram _____ 127

Twitter _____130

   How is Twitter Different? _____130

   Creating Your Twitter Profile _____ 131

   The Right Marketing Strategy _____ 134

   Measuring the Results _____140

   Advertising on Twitter _____ 141

LinkedIn _____ 146

   Setting Up Your LinkedIn Company Page 146

   The Perfect Strategy _____ 149

   Advertising on LinkedIn _____ 152

   Is Your Marketing Strategy Working? ___ 154

Pinterest _____ 156

   Using Pinterest for Business _____ 156

   Your Pinterest Strategy _____ 161

   Advertising on Pinterest _____ 163

   Pinterest Analytics _____ 167

Conclusion_____ 169

Introduction

Social Media Marketing is currently the most powerful tool that can help businesses (whether small or not) to reach customers and prospects. But with over 88 percent of all the companies marketing their businesses on at least one social media platform, you can see how easy can be for your brand to get lost in all that noise.

In order for your business social media pages to gain more organic exposure, reach to engaged brand advocates, and even drive more sales and leads, you will need a concise marketing strategy to rise to the top. Luckily for you, this book offers just that.

Peeling through the layers of the most popular social media platforms to get to the core of what makes an online marketing strategy successful, this book will teach you just how to promote your brand on social media.

Whether you are already active on social media or have never had a Facebook account, this book will guide your social media marketing plan every step of the way – from the creation of your account and optimizing your profile, through posting content that your audience will want to engage with, and all the way to advertising and promoting your brand for more traffic and followers.

Covering Facebook, YouTube, Instagram, Twitter, LinkedIn, and Pinterest, this guide will show you that social media marketing can bring success to your business, despite the fierce competition.

A strong social media presence is something your business cannot afford to miss out on. Read on to see how to create a killer social media marketing plan that will instantly drive thousands of followers to your profile.

The Importance of Social Media

Unless you have been living under a rock, chances are, you are more than familiar with the term *social media*. In fact, you probably have an active account on at least one of the popular social media platforms. For the sake of your time, I will not go into defining social media or bore you with its early rise. Instead, let's look at why is that social media is so important and how to take advantage of its popularity.

Easy and convenient connecting with friends and family aside, social media offers many other advantages that people in the past couldn't enjoy. From getting to know people from all over the world, to staying updated with the latest news, sharing your opinion, and discovering new things, products, and services, social media has become an inevitable part of the modern society of today. Growing with an insanely fast pace, the social networks are now one of the fastest growing industries in the world. It is no doubt that many businesses have taken advantage of the activity on social media and managed to increase their conversion.

If you think of social media as nothing but a trend that is doomed to fade away, you cannot be more wrong. With more and more people joining every day and using the social media platforms efficiently for various purposes, it is safe to say that the social media industry is definitely at its peak and will only grow bigger in the years to come.

If you want for your business to evolve, then forget about newspapers or TV ads, because right now, social media is the ticket for expanding your company.

Statistics Don't Lie

If I still haven't managed to convince you that marketing your business on the most popular social media platforms is the best business strategy for your product/service today, then perhaps these statistics will cast some light and help you realize that presenting your business on social media is the best way to reach your target audience.

As of 2019, there are 7.7 billion people in the world today. It is interesting to know that 4.2 billion of these people are internet users, but what's even more fascinating is the fact that more than 2.7 billion of the internet users are active on social media. That means that over 64% of the people that surf the internet spend some efficient time on social media. In fact, according to many studies done in

the past few years, the average time that people -
spend on social media is nearly 2 hours, or more
precisely, 117 minutes. No wonder why most of
the small businesses that are active on social media
post daily. Since statistics also say that there is a
new social media user practically every 10 seconds,
it is pretty obvious why signing up your business
for some social media activity can turn out to be
highly profitable.

Read on to see what social media marketing can
throw your way as well as to find out how to
successfully jumpstart the whole process.

Why My Business Needs Social Media?

At this point, not being present on social media is like flipping through a telephone book to find the number of your hairdresser. Or still owning a Nokia 3310. And while there is nothing wrong with using a two-decade-old cell phone model or keeping it old-school with hand-written telephone books, one thing is certain – those people miss out on the perks of today's technology. And that's perfectly fine. If you are just a guy who has a no-modern-technology principle, that is. But if you are a business that is looking for a way to increase the conversion and reap as many benefits as possible, then being present online is a must.

For many people social media is the internet, so they spend their hours scrolling down their social media platforms. Why? Because there is no reason to leave, actually. From chatting with people, to being up-to-date with news and finding and buying products and services, the social networks literally have it all. If you want your business to be successful, then having a strong social media presence is of great essence.

If your business is still not active on social media, then that is definitely the missing link that can strengthen the connection between your product/service and your customers. Still not sure whether it is worth the time and effort? Here are the benefits of being present on the social networks:

Web Traffic

Marketing your business on social media is a crucial part for your web traffic:

Posting on Social Media Drives Your Targeted Audience

Of course you want your business to be the first thing people will see when surfing the internet for similar products/services. But is that really possible if you are not active online? Posting regularly on social media will help you take domination over the first search page which will, in turn, increase your profits.

These social media posts are extremely valuable for increasing web traffic. For instance, think about what happens when you update your website. It surely takes a while for it to get traction with the search engines, right? That means that the number of customers that will be aware of your new content will be limited. Posting on social media will help your potential customers find your new content easily and then be re-directed to your website. This means that you don't have to wait for a customer to

11

click on your website to find out your updates. Social media allows you to reach potential customers even if they are not looking to buy at that exact moment,

Social Media Posts Boosts the SEO

Search engine optimization is of great importance for your online presence and overall business. Don't be fooled that this is not that important. SEO experts know which sites have constant traffic and which sits lonely and forgotten. A great content strategy can obviously skyrocket your search rankings, however, social media posts also have the power to drive more traffic to your site. By re-sharing popular content you can easily optimize your page and lure existing and potential customers to take a peek. The boosted traffic will then lead to inbound clicks and will have a significant impact on your prominence in Google rankings.

Quoting Can Make You More Reachable

Sometimes, a simple quote can throw more traffic your way. Whether you have used a PR tool such as HARO to find experts for your site or you simply want to quote an expert with a strong influence on social media, this can surely help your business. Chances are, by quoting (and tagging!) an expert in your tweet or Facebook post, that person will most likely share or retweet your post which will help you reach potential customers from their list of followers and increase your site's traffic.

Connecting with Customers

Being the bridge that can connect the gap between you and your customers, social media is definitely the shortcut you need to take in order to reach your audience the fastest way possible.

Reaching Customers

Social media is perhaps the only tool that can help you reach customers from all age groups at once. These networks are not just for teenagers searching for entertainment. The social media platforms are actively used by more than 2.7 billion people, so it is safe to say that whatever your target audience is, your potential customers are spending some efficient time on social media already. In fact, a study has actually found that 37% of all the Americans over 65 years of age are social media users.

Whether you want to reach young adults, housewives, or retirees, social media is the best place to introduce your product/service to them.

Besides, advertising on social media allows targeting and retargeting your audience which can play a crucial role in your marketing strategy. For instance, the ads on Facebook can be filtered around the needs of your customers and target only the age, location, industry, etc. of the audience that you are trying to reach.

Learning about Your Target Audience

Perhaps the biggest reason why social media marketing is so game-changing for businesses is the fact that these networks actually allow you to have a real interaction with your existing and potential customers. This creates an incredible opportunity to peek inside your audience's lives and learn about the customer behaviors first-hand. By reading posts and tweets, you can easily find the answers to the questions that every business is mostly concerned with:

- What product/services do people want to buy and why?

- What kind of websites do people mostly visit?

- What are the biggest hobbies nowadays and how can my product/service help?

- What types of posts do people share the most?

Finding the answers to these questions will help you understand your customers and allow you to write compelling posts and tweets that people will find appealing. By retweeting and sharing, you will not only increase the traffic and eventually profits, but also pinpoint what are the disappointments of the customers and how to refine your product/service in order to increase conversion.

Getting Noticed Easily

Imagine that you are hosting an event. A decent promotion is kind of required, right? What best way to do it than to have an active social media presence? Social media platforms will help you spread the word which will not only bring more guests, but can also throw a few big perks your way such as finding donors that are eager to participate.

Improving Your Brand's Image

Marketing your product/service on social media can help you thrive as a company, increase the exposure of your brand, and make its image recognizable and trustworthy.

The Best Customer Service Tool

Building a great image for your brand starts with keeping your customers happy and content. Many studies have shown that customers mostly reward those companies that take the time to quickly respond to their inquiries. But quickly responding to complaints isn't what it used to be. If there is a customer request pending, they are expecting for the issue to be solved right away.

Social media helps you offer customer service that is quick, helpful, and proactive, and gives you the opportunity to reach and help your customers before they get the chance to call your call center. This little trick just saved British Telecom over 2 million pounds in customer service costs, so just let that sink in for a second.

Building Up the Loyalty of Your Brand

This is actually pretty self-explanatory, but it would be remiss not to mention it. By taking the time to engage with your customers actively and provide them with beneficial info, help with inquiries, and keep them entertained without asking a thing in return, your brand's loyalty is actually enhanced.

The right social media presence can bring value to the customers and show them that you are not looking to empty their pockets, but that you actually care whether they are satisfied with your product/service or not.

Getting Started With Social Media Marketing

Posting family pictures and restaurant check-ins, does not actually make you a social media guru. Even if you have an active account that you use regularly, there are a lot more angles that need to be considered when looking to use social networks as a strong marketing tool. You need to stop looking at social media as a user, but as someone who is trying to reach all users.

Did you know that Instagram has its highest traffic between 9 and 11 am? Or that you can actually communicate on Twitter in six different ways? Do not skip this chapter thinking you are expert on social media, but read on to see how you can scratch the surface and find the best way to start your social media marketing.

Making Your Social Media Marketing Plan

In order to slay the competition and help your business thrive on social media, good planning ahead is indeed required. Your approach to social media marketing must take into consideration the real picture of the market, the needs of your target audience, but also the wants and needs of your business. If you don't know where to start and how to craft your ideal strategy, these steps will most likely help you design a decent plan:

#1: Check Your Social Media Presence

If you are not just starting out, then chances are your business is already present on some of the social media platforms. Before you create a strategy and head somewhere, take a good look at your networks and review where you are currently standing:

- Which platforms are you present on?

- Are your profiles optimized?

- Is some network bringing you value already?

- What do your profiles look like when compared to the competition?

If you are not present on social media, the next chapters will help you create killer accounts. But before you do that, peek into the competitors' profiles to see what they are currently offering.

#2: Define Your Ideal Customer

Someone said that the main goal of marketing is to know exactly what your customers need in order for the product to practically sells itself. Keep that in mind when thinking about your ideal customers. You will need to get pretty specific if you want to avoid marketing to the wrong kind of audience.

Before you actually start marketing, you will need to know exactly who your customer is. Here is a great example of how your customers should be defined: *A stay-at-home mom between 25 and 40 years of age who lives in the United States, lives in a house in the suburbs, primarily uses Instagram and has a thing for crafting activities.*

To define the buyer persona that your product/service is created for, answer the following questions:

- Age

- Location

- Job Title and Income

- Interests

- Pain Points (that can be solved by the usage of your product/service)

- Most Used Social Network

#3: Have a Social Media Marketing Mission Line

This may seem silly to some, but having a mission statement can help you stay focused and keep your eye on the ball at all times. This is what will actually drive all of your actions, so make sure that you come up with a good one. A great mission line should explain what your primary goal is, and what you are hoping to get out of social media marketing.

For instance, a good social media marketing mission statement should say: *"To use the social media platforms to help people learn about healthy eating, offer healthy and nutritious free recipes, and promote my new books."*

Of course, this is just an example. Your mission statement can be whatever you are trying to achieve through marketing. The main point is to make sure that all of your posts and tweets align with that statement. If you post randomly and without any guiding goal, your marketing strategy will be doomed to fail.

#4: Decide on Your Metrics

For your social media marketing to be successful, you will have to have a decent measuring strategy. If you don't measure your posts the right way, you will fail to improve your marketing, and may even end up losing customers. That's why a good measuring plan is important.

How will you decide whether your social media marketing strategies are successful? What will the key success metrics be? What is important to you? Here are some metrics that can help you whether you are marketing your products/servicer the right way:

- Total Shares

- Conversion Rate

- Total Mentions of Your Brand

- Time Spent on Your Website

- Reach

- Sentiment

#5: Think About Investing in Social Media Management

If you are planning on marketing on various platforms and be super-active on social media in order to reap the benefits, then chances are that you will be crunched for time. That means that you might not be able to measure and track the progress of your social media marketing strategies. In order for you to stay up-to-date with the things that your customers like the most (as well as what they don't appreciate) so you can improve and provide more value, you need to have a social media management tool to increase your productivity.

Depending on your needs, there are various tools to choose from. https://hootsuite.com/, https://sproutsocial.com/ and https://buffer.com/ offer some great options. Choose the right pricing and plan your investment in these tools accordingly.

The Best 5 Social Media Marketing Strategies to Increase Productivity

Whether you call them strategies, habits, or just a way of marketing on social media, there are some things that you need to take care of in order to dust off your lonely business social channel. Or develop a successful routine, in case your business is new to the social media world, that is.

Strategy #1: Set Your Scheme and Stick to It

If you do not have a thought out strategy, your posts and tweets will probably just go unnoticed. Besides your objectives, which should already be firmly set, you also need to have a good course of action about how you will actually get to your primarily goal.

Choosing what and when to post is a good example of an organized scheme. You should have a set limit of how many posts you think about publishing daily. Decide on your strategy, and stick to it. Of course, you will adjust this on the go, but the most important thing is to keep yourself organized and punctual.

Scheduling posts is, obviously, just one example. In the following chapters you will come across many schemes for successful social media marketing that you should take advantage of.

Strategy #2: Post Regularly and Be Consistent

In order to keep your customers interested in your product or service, you will have to have a good posting strategy. Providing regular content is a great marketing strategy as it helps your customers stay updated, plus it shows that you are always looking for ways to improve and provide even more value. However, as important as regular content is, it will be pretty useless if you do not have a consistent approach.

The best way to provide regular content and to maintain its consistency is if you know exactly what your audience is looking for. Do your homework well before hitting the "share" button.

Strategy #3: Approach Your Social Media Channels Differently

Despite the fact that you are marketing the same product/service, you need to keep in mind that you are actually doing it on different social media platforms. What does that mean? That means that you cannot simply copy and paste your posts. Why? Because different platforms usually means different audience. Many of Instagram followers will not be LinkedIn users and vice versa.

For instance, LinkedIn is more business-oriented and its content is a bit more serious and educational than, for example, Instagram, which it has users who are mostly looking for appealing and vivid visual posts.

Treat your social media channels as different entities and keep the post separated and, most importantly, unique. Even if you are looking to spread the same message, make sure you adjust it for the different types of audience.

Strategy #4: Stay Engaged

Engagement is all that social media is about. It is a process of keeping in touch, listening, and painting the picture that your audience actually want to see. Social media marketing is not marketing if you are not 100% engaged. And not only with your posts and shares, but with answering, retweeting, and responding to complaints, as well. Your customers need to know that you care about them, and if you are not engaged, well, your other strategies will also be pretty useless.

The best way to make the audience notice your engagement is to keep them involved at all times. Ask for their opinion, make questionnaires, come up with unique competitions, offer rewards, discounts, etc. Keeping your business connected to your customers is the secret behind every successful marketing strategy.

Strategy #5: Act like a Human

Social media is all about the human interaction, not pitches and logos. This can be somewhat tricky when you are just starting your social media marketing journey as most companies make their initial approach a hard selling point. Avoid putting off potential and existing customers with customer reviews, product introductions, and purchasing codes. Instead, make your approach as friendly as possible.

But do not implement this only in the beginning. Your business should find a way to always act like a person (to some degree, of course), not to approach customers as an entity.

Killer Content is the Key

Like any other marketing strategy, if your social media marketing doesn't have any returns, then you are investing the wrong way. And your investment on social media is the content you post.

Your customers expect you to bring value. If your posts are not valuable then it is pretty impossible to keep the audience engaged. After all, it is the content that drives traffic to your page. In order for your social media marketing to turn out beneficial, you will need to know exactly what types of content to share and why. And yes, there is more than one way of sharing.

User-Generated Content

The content that is produced by unpaid contributors is called user-generated content. This makes perfect sense if you think about it, since it is in our nature to try new products/services based on other people's recommendations in order to avoid making mistakes or disappointing ourselves. There are more chances that we will respond positively to a photo shared by a friend than a photo shared by a brand.

This type of content will not only bring authenticity to your brand, but it will also connect your company to your customers in a more human way.

GIFS

GIF is a very popular image type that supports both, static and animated images. This image type is especially attractive to younger population thanks to its interesting visual elements. Choosing to add GIFs to your page will give a message to your audience (whatever age group they belong to) that you follow recent trends and that you actually listen.

If you want to keep your customers captivated and stimulated visually, then adding GIFs is the right choice.

Infographics

If you have to discuss a more complex subject but don't want to bore your customers with heavy and dull reading, then graphics are the perfect decision. Properly designed graphics cannot only simplify a complicated topic, but will also attract the customer's eye, even if they are not really interested in the particular subject. Infographics are an extremely valuable tool for your social media marketing, so make sure to incorporate them whenever you get the chance.

Concept Visualization

Infographics are great and super effective, but only if you are not trying to tell a really long story. Otherwise, it is pretty hard to design them in a way that will cover enough info and keep the customer's attention. Another powerful tool for simplifying complex topics is concept visualization.

Concept visualization are all those graphs, charts, and visuals that are basically self-explanatory. Here, by illustrating a single idea you can present your story in a smaller, fun, and a much more absorbable way. Besides, they are more shareable than infographics which makes them perfect for your social media marketing.

Live Streaming

Live streaming is a great way to lure traffic into your page, but that is not the only reason. While you are streaming and gaining more views, you can also add additional info about your service or product and actually know that people are reading it. Besides, live streaming is also great for interacting with your customers through some Q&As and learning about what they want first hand.

Facebook

Assuming that you already know how big Facebook is, I will not try to convince you why you need to open a Facebook account. Besides, when you say it like that, *your business needs a Facebook page*, it sounds like a pretty obvious understatement. But I will give you a taste of the newest statistics and make you understand why having a decent marketing strategy on Facebook can be of huge importance for your overall business.

Although Facebook has been a big deal practically since the day it was invented, its marketing side now offers tools that we didn't think were even possible 10 years ago. From selling services via your chatbot and promoting your product in a 360-degree video, Facebook marketing is a standard that all businesses must meet.

The fact that Facebook has 2.27 billion active users, from which 1.49 billion use this platform actively on daily basis, is a pretty good reason why you should seriously invest in marketing your brand on Facebook. When the average person spends 50 minutes per day on this platform, you can only imagine how huge of a marketplace this network can be.

And while it is true that Facebook is one crowded marketplace, not taking advantage of the tools that it offers can be a terrible mistake for your business. Being as huge as it is, the odds are, your competition is already out there, promoting their products on this platform. Sitting this out is simply not something that your business can afford. It may seem scary, but if done correctly and with just the right amount of effort, you too could have amazing returns. Let this chapter guide your way for a successful marketing journey.

Creating Your Facebook Page

First things first, in order to market on Facebook, you must have a Facebook page up and running. By doing that, you will be joining 60 million businesses from all over the world that are promoting their brands on this platform. It sounds intimidating, I know, but that's why this step is so important. Creating a killer page can really make a huge difference in the whole marketing process. Before you start posting quality content, you need to have a personalized page, first.

If you already have a personal account, then you probably know how this works. Pages for businesses are what profile pages are for people. People connect with people by 'adding' them as friends, and follow businesses by 'liking' their pages. Why am I mentioning this? If you, by any chance, decide to open a profile for your business instead of a page, Facebook may shut it down permanently since it's against their rules.

To start this process, go to https://www.facebook.com/pages/creation/. There, you will see two different categories to choose from:

1. Business or Brand

2. Community or Public Figure

Assuming you are a business, click on **'Get Started'** under **'Business or Brand'** to start the process. The first thing you will need to do is enter the name of the Page. Think about this carefully as it is the name that people will see. There should be an option for you to change the URL, but nevertheless, choose wisely.

After you've chosen your name, you should choose the category that your business falls under. Fill out the details such as address, phone number, etc. and click on **'Continue'**.

As simple as that, you will be redirected to your new page. Follow Facebook's tips for customizing your page.

Profile Picture

The first step you need to take care of is to add a profile picture for your business. Think of this picture as your business' identity and make sure it is something that represents your company well, like a well-designed logo. Your profile picture is the first impression that your business gives on Facebook, so make sure it is recognizable.

It is recommended to upload a photo with 180 x 180 pixels, but do not worry if you don't have a square photo. Facebook will suggest cropping, but the important thing is that your entire logo (if uploading a logo) fits into the cropped picture.

Cover Photo

Your cover photo, the horizontal image that is found on the top of your page, in addition to your profile picture, is what gives personality to your page. Businesses usually use this photo to promote special offerings, discounts, etc.

To upload your cover photo just click the **'Add a cover photo'** button from your welcome menu. The best dimensions are 851 x 315 pixels, but again, you can adjust your photo directly on Facebook.

You can (and should!) update your cover photo on regular basis. To do so, just click the **'Change**

Cover' button found in the lower corner on the right of your current cover.

Description

To let people know what your business is all about, you will need a thoughtfully-written couple of sentences to introduce your brand. Facebook allows the maximum of 155 characters so choose your words carefully. Keep in mind that this description will also appear in the search results so make sure it is creatively descriptive.

Username

The username is the name that appears in your Facebook URL so help customers find you more easily. You have only 50 characters for your username; make sure to use them for something unique that is not already being used by other companies.

Setting Up the Roles

Now that the foundation of your page has been completed, it is time to set up the roles. The best thing about business pages is that they are kept completely separate from your personal Facebook account. That means that you are not the only person who can edit the page. Other people from your organization can also maintain the page without having to log in through your personal account. However, it is up to you to assign the roles.

Admin. The admin of the page manages pretty much everything. From sending messages, responding to comments, publishing and deleting posts, to advertising and even assigning the roles. This person should be someone you trust the most, so choose carefully.

Editor. Pretty much all permission as the admin, without the ability to assign roles.

Moderator. Moderators can respond and delete comments, but do not have the permission to post on the page. They are permitted to advertise on Facebook, though.

Advertiser. As the name suggests, the advertiser is only in charge of the advertising part.

Analyst. They are only allowed to track the posts and see which admin published what.

Live Contributor. The live contributor is someone that can go live (when live streaming), but does not have the permission to publish or respond to comments.

Call-to-Action

Call to action is a great benefit that Facebook provides. As of December 2014, Facebook allows Pages to include a CTA button, which is a very convenient way for customers to take action with your business. Click on **'Add a Button'** found above your cover and choose what the button should allow customers to do: get in touch, download an app, purchase a product, donate, book your services, etc. then add a link to direct them to your website, video, or another landing page.

Page Tabs

In order for you to organize the content that customers will see on your Page, it is recommended that you add custom tabs. That way your audience will have the chance to see your photos, check for open jobs, go to your website, visit your Pinterest, etc.

In your left navigation, there is a **'Manage Tabs'** button. Click on it to change your tabs.

Verify

Customers do not trust unverified pages, it's as simple as that. This is not absolutely required, but if you want to add more value to your page and include a degree of authority, it is recommended.

Go to **'Settings'** ➔ **'General'** ➔ **'Page Verification'** to enter your phone number, country, etc. You will get a Facebook verification code to enter.

Getting Your Fans

Now that your Page is up and running, it is time for you to get your first likes. Getting a 'like' from a customer is them saying they are interested in what you are selling and that they want to keep in touch with your products/services and promotions. As the most successful business have millions of likes, your goal is to strive to get as many of those 'thumbs-ups' as possible.

Why Not Just Buy Likes?

It seems easier and more convenient, right? If you type "buying Facebook likes" on Google, you will be redirected to sites upon sites all selling packages of likes for a fixed price. You may be tricked into thinking that this will make your business look more successful and credible, but those likes are nothing but thin air. These so-called companies that sell these types of likes use fake or compromised accounts and click farms. You will not be getting actual likes from an audience that is interested in your product/service. It is really unlikely that any of them with engage with your content, so the only thing that buying them will get you is empty likes.

Promoting On Facebook

In order to get your likes, you need to make sure that you are actually promoting your Page on Facebook the right way. Here are some tips that will help you gain likes:

- Make sure your username and Page name is clear

- Go through the 'About' section and optimize. Include relevant keywords that will help people find you easier on Google and other search engines

- Share your Page with your friends and get them to like it

- Finally, be active and interact with the fans that you already have, as they will drive more traffic to your page

Promoting Through Your Website

If you are new to Facebook but have a website that already has a group of customers, do not forget to spread the word and promote your Facebook page there. You don't have to convince them to do so; adding a page plugin on your website with built-in Facebook iframe code will allow your audience to like or even share your page without actually leaving your website.

Promoting Directly to Your Customers

Another great way of promoting your Facebook page is directly to your customers. Have a store? Design a fabulous Facebook sticker with your logo on it to know people you are online. When sending emails to your customers, include your page's URL at the top corner of the message. You can also include the URL on your receipts. Want to get even more creative? Why not announce a promotion where you will offer discounted prices in return for a like on the spot.

Posting Like a Pro

We have already discussed the importance of quality posts. Your content is the core of social media marketing and as such, it should be posted regularly. Think of the posts as food for your Page. The more you feed it, the bigger it grows. But just as the food you eat, your posts should also be of high quality and carefully selected.

Besides the different types of content that we talked about earlier, there are also different ways to post on social media. Here are the different ways in which you can share your content with the world via Facebook:

Facebook Images

Studies have shown that Facebook image posts are 2.3 times more appealing and engaging to the audience, so that's a pretty good reason why you should share some quality images with your customers.

To post an image on Facebook is simple, simply click on **'Share a Photo or Video'** below the blank post space. Alternatively, you can start typing into the blank post and then click on the camera button on the left to upload your image.

The size of the images you are going to post is not that important (although 1200 x 3600 pixels is recommended). What's more important is the ratio. Make sure your ratio is 1.9:1 for best results.

Facebook Links

The best way to feed your Page is to share links to your products/services. Whether you are writing cooking blog posts or sell toys, your Facebook page needs to have links of your recent product/service in order for your customers to stay updated.

You can post a link the same way you post a written post. Just paste the link into the blank post space, and then write a short and engaging description. But wait before hitting 'Share' just yet.

To make your Page look more professional, avoid keeping the URLs. Once the link has been uploaded, delete the URL so that your post looks clean.

Facebook Video

Did you know that it is predicted that Facebook will soon be all video? That's no surprise really since the number of daily video views is higher than 8 billion. There are over 100 million hours of Facebook videos that are watched every day. These are some powerful statistics that show us just how engaging videos are to people on Facebook.

To post a video, the process is the same as posting a photo. Click the **'Share a Photo or Video'** and then simply select the desired file from your computer. The recommended file format is MP4 and MOV. Then, add a line or two of text, describing or introducing the video to your audience.

Keep in mind that Facebook plays the first 5-10 seconds automatically, which means that even if a person is not thinking about watching a video, when scrolling down their news feed, they will see the beginning of your video. Try to make the beginning as appealing as possible in order to lure people to hit the play button and watch the whole thing.

Facebook Live

Unlike posting pre-produced videos, Facebook live is a feature that allows you to stream live videos via your smartphone. To give this a try, open the Facebook app on your phone and go to your Page. Click the **'Publish'** button and then choose the **'Live Video'** option. Once you allow Facebook to access your camera and microphone, select **'Continue'**.

Before you actually start streaming, you need to enter some privacy settings. You can choose whether to stream to friends, the whole public or just to yourself. Once you choose that, you should write a line or two compelling people to watch your video. The line will go alongside your streaming, so make sure it is unique and descriptive.

When ready to roll, hit **'Go Live'** and voila... You are on the air.

When you are done streaming, select **'Finish'.** This will end the streaming but will keep a recording on your Page for later watching.

Bu connecting with the audience this way, you show them that you care not only about making a profit, but also about their opinion and satisfaction. Engaging with your customers through Facebook Live can turn out to be a great marketing trick.

Facebook Instant Articles

Just like suggested in its name, Facebook Instant Articles means reading articles on the spot, without having to leave Facebook and be redirected to another site. This feature is great because it saves time and it is pretty convenient.

Not all businesses can take advantage of Instant Articles, but if you happen to be a publisher, this can throw a lot of good things your way.

Virtual Reality

Virtual reality for Facebook is something that you absolutely have to try if you have a mesmerizing story to tell. And if you need to promote a special place or an important experience of some kind, then you really cannot afford to pass out on this feature. Facebook Virtual Reality allows you to post 360-degrees videos for a full enjoyment. This works best on mobile and it is the most appreciated if recorded with a 360-degree camera, so think about investing in a Ricoh Theta or Allie camera as a part of your killer marketing strategy.

PIN YOUR POSTS

Pinning your posts means choosing the order in which they will appear on your page. Facebook offers an option to pin a post to the top of your page so that your most important announcements/promotions are the first thing that attracts the customer's eye when they visit your Page.

Try this out by clicking on the arrow found on the top right corner of a post you have previously shared. Then, simply click on **'Pin to Top of Page'.** Until you pin another post, this is the post that will be shown at the top of your Page.

Optimizing for SEO

If you are wondering whether your Facebook Page can affect your Google ranking, stop, because it does. And I am sure it has a way bigger impact than what you can imagine. Here is the role that a successful Facebook Page can play in Search Engine Optimization (SEO):

- It can drive traffic to your website

- It can attract a highly relevant audience interested in what you are selling

- It builds links through your Facebook shares

- It can improve your visibility with the help of optimized keywords

And if you are still not sure how this process works, here is an example:

1. You post your content on Facebook *(provide value)*

2. Your customers share your posts *(building links)*

3. The friends of your friends notice your content *(boosting visibility)*

4. The friends of your friends then click to see the content *(higher click-through rates)*

5. More people visit your website *(higher traffic)*

6. More people engage with your business *(low bounce rate)*

This simple example clearly shows you the importance of Facebook Marketing for your ranking on the search engines.

Keywords, Keywords, Keywords

Your Facebook content can be successfully optimized by using relevant keywords. You may have noticed how Google also lists social media results when searching for keywords. For instance, if you type *organic cotton clothing company,* you will get results for websites and social media networks of the top organic cotton clothing companies. That is because these companies have optimized their Pages and websites and included the relevant keywords *organic, cotton, clothing,* and *company,* which is how you will actually find them online.

Optimizing your content on Facebook will help people discover you and learn about your business easily. But how can you do that? There are three different ways in which you can add proper keywords and improve your business' visibility:

#1: Optimize Your URL

Make sure that your Page's URL contains the keywords that people will most likely use to search for your business online.

#2: Optimize Your 'About' Section

You may not know this, but what you write under 'About' on Facebook can also help people discover you online. Here is how you can ensure that your 'About' section is optimized:

- Conduct research to see what are the most relevant keywords for your business

- Choose 2 of the most relevant keywords

- Write your description creatively, mentioning these keywords a few time

- Make sure your Business Info is completed. Often times business' Pages are not listed at the top of Google Results because of lack of details. Make sure to enter your exact location, phone number, website, and other important info that will help customers find you.

Tip: Stay natural! Your description should contain the relevant keywords but at the same time sound warm and appealing. Do not go overboard with the keywords you find.

#3: Optimize the Post You Share

This is perhaps the trickiest part as the attempt to optimize your posts should be continuous and implemented on each post you think about sharing.

Just like your 'About' section, your post should also contain relevant keywords. For instance, if you are promoting a new product, conduct research to see what the most relevant keywords for that kind of products are, and include them in your post. If you are not an SEO guru, then you should seriously think about hiring an expert to have at your disposal.

The Right Marketing Strategy

And now, let's talk some real business. Now that you know what your posts should look like and how to optimize them for best results, it is time for the real challenge of Facebook marketing – finding the right strategy, or in other words, what and when to post.

Assuming that you already know who your audience is, let's move forward and talk some real strategies.

*If you don't know the persona of your audience, you can use a tool called **Audience Insights**. This amazing tool will help you obtain behavioral, as well as demographic data of your audience, in order to determine what kind of posts people are actually looking for.*

Social Media Content Calendar

If you are not using a social media management tool, then you absolutely need to have a content calendar for your Facebook posts. It doesn't have to be anything fancy. Your content calendar can be a simple spreadsheet where you will write your posts in advance and appoint them for different times.

Here are some tips for a great Social Media Content Calendar:

- Have tabs for each of your platforms (This calendar is not only for Facebook but your other Social Media Networks as well)

- Have a day-by-day post plan that is divided into time slots

- Leave some columns for specific details such as the name of the campaign, images you wish to post alongside, the count of characters, a short note to remember, etc.

- In order to keep track of large campaigns, leave room for a monthly view of your posts

Scheduling Your Posts

Although having a social media calendar can be a real life-saver when it comes to social media marketing, you will never be able to take a break if you do not actually schedule your posts on Facebook. If you plan on successfully marketing on this platform, you will need to be super-active and post regularly. That can be tricky if you are crunched for time and not always available. Thankfully, Facebook offers a great option that allows you to schedule your posts ahead of time.

The process is pretty simple. Instead of hitting **'Publish'** and sharing your post after it has been written, click on the arrow found next to **'Publish'** and select **'Schedule'** instead. Enter the time and date, and you are all set.

If you have a change of hearts, do not worry, you can always reschedule or cancel. Just click on **'Publishing Tools'** that's found at the top of your Page and choose to *Reschedule, Cancel Schedule, Backdate,* or *Delete.*

When to Post and How Often?

Scheduling your posts is great, but if you do not actually know when the right time for posting is, it may not turn out to be that beneficial. So, when is the right time to post on Facebook? And how often should you share your posts?

If you came here looking for a clear-cut answer that will apply to your business, let me break it to you – there isn't one. When and how often to post on Facebook depends on many factors: whether you audience is in the same time zone, your location, your main goal, what your business is about, etc. However, there are some tricks to have up your sleeve.

Stick to the Rules of Thumb

WHEN TO POST:

- The rule of a thumb is that your posts will be seen by more people if you shoot for between 1 p.m. and 5 p.m. on weekdays, and between noon and 1 p.m. on the weekends.

- The best days for posting on Facebook are Saturday and Sunday, followed by Friday and Thursday, so save your most important posts for these days.

- People seem to be happier on Fridays, so save your cheerful and upbeat posts for this day.

- Statistics say that posting on Facebook at 3 p.m. will get you the most likes, while the 1 p.m. posts will bring you more shares, so have this in mind when posting.

HOW OFTEN TO POST:

When it comes to how often your posts should be, the rule of a thumb is between 1 and 2 posts per day. You may think that posting frequently will bring more engagement, but it is quite the opposite, actually. Studies have shown that frequent posts bring a decrease in audience.

Another rule of a thumb is that posting more than 1-2 times a day can be beneficial only for the successful companies that have more than 10,000 followers. Posting more than 2 times a day for companies that have less than 10,000 likes can bring 60% fewer clicks, statistics show.

You need to remember that quality trumps always trumps quantity, so do not obsess yourself with how frequent your posts should be. Instead, make sure that your content is well-crafted, created for the right audience, and consistent.

Facebook Bots

A bot is an AI program that people communicate with in order to ask for some info or automatically complete a certain task. Facebook bots have completely taken over the Messenger and are especially important for businesses.

The same way people use Messenger to chat with friends, they can also use this platform to communicate with bots in order to ask for updates, change a shipping address, ask for working hours, order items, etc. By getting rid of never-ending scrolling down the company's page in order to find what they are looking for, communicating with bots makes the shopping experience much more convenient for customers. In fact, half of the people are interested in shopping from an artificial bot, so make sure you add a chatbot to your Facebook Page.

There are a lot of platforms that can help you create a chatbot. Chatfuel.com is one of the most popular ones.

Generating Leads

Leads are potential customers. They are those people that have already shown interest in your product or service but are not paying customers just yet. For instance, if someone has subscribed for a free trial, have downloaded a free chapter of your eBook, or has signed up for a demo product, that person is a *lead.*

In order for you to actually turn your leads into customers, you need to have a good strategy about how to generate leads and post content that they will find attractive:

- Posting landing pages for special offers

- Scheduling Facebook events for an upcoming webinar

- Creating and posting videos that will advertise special lead generation offers

- Posting Facebook Lives in order to remind your audience for upcoming events

- Share blog posts that have already proven to generate leads

Of course, you need to be careful not to overdo it. Not all of your content should be lead generation. Mix things up and come up with the right balance that works best for your business.

Facebook Lead Ads can be used in order to gather Facebook lead info. This is a great feature that will grant access of your special offers to your audience, without the need to leave the Facebook app.

Tracking Your Results

Now that you know a few tricks that can get you more clicks, likes, and shares, it is time to learn how you can check to see if your marketing efforts really pay out. Your marketing strategy will not a proper plan for tracking the results will involve a lot of guesses and maybes, which can result in underachievement.

For that purpose, Facebook has created a great tool call *Facebook Insights* that can help you analyze, track, and measure your success.

To enter this tool, select the **'Insights'** tab that is found at the top of your page. Once you do that you will be brought to the **'Overview'** of your Page, which is your Page's activity for the last week. You can take a look at this, but if you want to check out some more specific details, you will need to go through the tabs on the left.

Likes. The Like section will show you how many likes you've received so far for each day. You will see a graph that will show your performance. There you will find the **Net Likes** graph, which is what you should be interested in most, and that is the number of likes minus the number of unlikes.

Reach. If you want to see how people engage with your content, check out the **Reach** tab. There you will find a graph of post engagement that is divided into organic traffic (traffic that occurs naturally) and paid traffic (the traffic that you pay for and target directly to specific consumers through advertising).

Page Views. This will not only show you the number of times your page has been visited, but also how those people got to your Page. Additionally, here, you can also learn about what people usually do after landing on your Page.

Posts. This is probably the most useful option that this tool offer, as it helps you learn about when your followers are online, which can be super helpful during your process of scheduling posts. **Posts** show your fans reactions, comments, shares, post hides, reports or spams, engagement rate, etc.

If you want a quick check of the success of your posts without having to go through Page Insights, simply click on **'People Reached'** that is find right above the **'Like'** button, and you can go through post details immediately.

Advertising on Facebook

To advertise your products or services on Facebook, you have to complete a process of three different elements:

1. Campaign

2. Ad Sets

3. Ads

This chapter will help you learn all about Facebook advertising and how to maximize the results with the minimum budget and effort.

Facebook Ad Campaign

Before you begin the process of creating an ad, Facebook will ask you to select your editor of choice, which will be Ad Manager or Power Editor. They both have their ups and downs, depending on what you are looking for. The Ad Manager is used the most as it is more versatile, but if you are a large company and looking for increased precision and control over multiple campaigns, then Power Editor may be a better fit.

For this purpose, let's imagine that you are satisfied with Ad Manager. In the right upper corner of your Page there is a drop-down menu. Click on it, and then select **'Create Ads'.**

There, you will be prompted to choose an objective for your campaign. You will find 11 objectives in total, divided into 3 categories. Choose the one that suits you the most. The initial process of starting a campaign has been completed.

The Ad-Sets

Once the initial process is over, you should then go through the steps of defining your audience, setting the budget, and scheduling and optimizing the ad set.

Audience

If you have used this tool before, chances are your audience is already remembered by Facebook. If not, enter specified info like gender, age, location, and language of your target audience. After that, you can add more filters by, for instance, targeting only the audience that has liked a specific page, or something like that.

Make sure that it is the **'Automatic Placements'** selected under **'Placements'.**

Budget

There are two budget typed to choose from:

Daily Budget – If your goal is to advertise continuously, then choose this option. Enter the amount that you are comfortable with spending on daily basis for this specific ad.

Lifetime Budget – Choose this option if you have a specified amount of time that you wish to run the ad for. Here, your budget will be spread evenly for that time period.

Schedule

Now it's time to schedule your ad set. You can either choose to start the advertising process immediately or schedule a start and end date for your ad.

Optimization

Click the **'Show Advanced Options'** button and choose your preferred optimization. Here, you choose the option that you want your advertisement to be optimized for so that Facebook can show the add to people that will pay attention the most.

If you are all set, click **'Continue'**

Creating the Ad

Now it is time to select the format, text, media, and links, and create your Facebook ad:

1. First of all, choose your desired format options. Facebook will show you suggestions (carousel, single image, slideshow, single video, etc.) so select the one that looks the most appealing to you.

2. Now that you have selected the look of your ad, upload the assets and write a captivating ad headline. Facebook will give recommendations for the design based on the selected format.

3. Tweak, polish, preview, and finally, finish the creation.

Tips for Successful Advertising

Here are some tips that can boost your advertisement process and, in turn, boost both the organic ad paid traffic:

Focus on Videos

Video ads bring far more clicks than the image-based ones. How-to videos, customer-testimonial videos, and tasteful product demonstration videos can help you generate a lot of business.

Go for Lookalike Audience

A lookalike audience is a group of people that is very similar to another group. This is a great advertisement trick, as you can actually create a list of customers (or even leads) and upload that to Facebook to create your lookalike audience. To upload this, go to your Ad Manager, open **'Audiences'** and choose the **'Lookalike Audience'** option.

When Retargeting, Be Specific

When retargeting your audience, do not just retarget them as a group, but try to get as specific as possible. Depending on what you are advertising, try to choose, for instance, only those people that have visited a specific part of your website, or purchased a specific type of product.

Install the Facebook Pixel

Facebook Pixel, the key tool for Facebook advertising, is a simple code that you place on your website that collects the data and enables you not only to keep a track of your conversions, but also to build audiences, optimize your ads, and even remarket.

To create your Facebook Pixel, go to your **'Facebook Events Manager'** and choose **'Pixels'**. Then, click on **'Create a Pixel'**, enter the name of your Pixel, and click on **'Create'.**

To add the Pixel to your website, you will need to install some codes on your website, but that mainly depends on the platform you use.

If you are using an e-commerce platform, this can be done easily as Facebook will offer you a Help article that will explain the whole process.

If you are working with a developer, you can choose the option to **Email Instructions to Developer.**

You can also choose to **Manually Install the Code Yourself**, in which case you will need to copy and paste the code into your website's header code.

Try the Callout Method

It may sound clichéd, but calling out for people's attention seems to be a trick that's as old as time. But who cares as long as it works? Try to start the ad with a couple of questions that will call out your audience.

For instance, if you are promoting your weight-loss book, you may want to start like this: "Tired of eating bland greens for the sake of your flat belly? Want to have both- a satisfied tummy and a lean figure? I have the perfect solution for you…" and then add a couple of words that describe your book.

Another perk of this method is that it can serve as an additional tool for targeting audience. Here, for example, the target audience are those people whose diets are inefficient, who are always hungry and miserable and are looking for a better way to lose weight. Which is exactly what you are offering.

Stick to the 20%-or-Less Text Rule

It was a Facebook's rule to automatically disapprove those image ads that had more than 20 percent of text. They might not be so strict anymore and sometimes even allow such ads, however, it is a fact that people respond better to the visual. Try to keep the text to a minimum by choosing the right words carefully, and make the image the star of your advertisement.

The Boost Post

Although not exactly an advertising strategy, the **'Boost Post'** option that Facebook offers is another great way in which you can, well, boost your post.

When to use this? Unless you are a super successful company with millions of fans, chances are you need to press the 'Boost Post' from time to time. When your post does not drag enough traffic to your page, it is time to use additional tools to boost your organic reach. The 'boost post' button will not only help you increase your organic traffic, but it will also give you the opportunity to reach a wider audience.

Of course, boosting your post and promoting it on Facebook will cost you some money. But if you think that it'll break the bank, you cannot be more wrong. Just like with Facebook ads, you get to set your own budget, so in the end, you pay the amount that you are actually comfortable with. The minimum amount is $1 per week, but keep in mind that the more money you spend, the wider your targeted audience will be.

Step 1: Choose Your Post

Whether it is the one you are crafting at the moment or an earlier post, choose the one you want to present to your audience and hit the **'Boost Post'** button that is found in the lower right corner of your post of your choice.

Step 2: Target Your Audience

After choosing the post you wish to boost, Facebook will give you the option to choose options for targeting the right audience for you. You can easily create a custom audience by selecting the **'Create New Audience'** option and defining it as you would like by setting the age range, location, specific interests, and other important factors.

Step 3: Set Your Budget

After defining your audience, you should have a pretty realistic idea of how much you need to spend for your boosted post. Again, you can spend the minimum of $1, but know that higher budget equals to higher reach.

Step 4: Set the Duration

You will then need to select the number of days you want your post to be boosted. The default is set for 1, 7, and 14 days, but you can also enter a specified date.

Step 5: Preview the Boosted Post

Now is the time for you to take a look at your ad and make sure that everything looks good (links work, it is error-free, etc.) as this is your last chance to correct any mistakes before your post actually goes live.

Step 6: Choose Your Payment Option

Choose the method in which you are planning to pay for your boost posts. Fill out the details and click **'Continue'.**

Step 7: Boost

Finally, you are ready to boost. To check the status of the post you have boosted, you can check out the **'Delivery'** column under **'Ads Manager'**

YouTube

I am certain that everyone who has ever used the Internet is aware of how huge YouTube is. In fact, I am also pretty sure that, at some point, we have all wasted an entire lazy day watching funny YouTube videos. But what not everyone knows is that, besides its ability to entertain, this platform has also become a crucial tool for successful marketers from all over the world.

With over 1.8 billion monthly users (who are actually logged-in), over 1 billion of hours of watched videos per day, and over 400 hours' worth of video being uploaded every minute, YouTube is the 2nd largest search engine.

Whatever category they might fall under, chances are, a huge chunk of your target audience is already on YouTube. Marketing your content on YouTube is a smart move that will help your brand grow by providing more value to your customers.

Creating Your Business Profile

Before we jump right to setting up your business YouTube Account and creating your profile, we first need to make sure that you have an active Google account. As you may know, YouTube is owned by Google, and by owning a Gmail account you can access YouTube logged-in.

But wait before opening YouTube and beginning the profile creation process. Tying up your YouTube profile to your already existing mail may not be such a good idea, especially if we are talking about your business Gmail account. Sharing your access to your YouTube profile with everyone in your company who has access to your business email is not that recommended. For that purpose, it is smart to open a different Gmail account:

1. Go to www.google.com and select the **'Sign In'** button found in the upper right corner.

2. Go to **'Create'** → **'Create Account'**.

3. Fill out the details by entering your name, the name of the email, password, birthday, etc. and click on **'Next Step'**.

4. Verify your account by entering your phone number where a code number will be sent. Type in the code and click **'Continue'**. Your new Gmail account is now up and running.

Now that you have a Gmail account, it is time to set up the actual YouTube account for your brand and create its profile.

To get started, simply, visit www.youtube.com. If you are logged in with your Gmail, then you are probably already logged in with YouTube. If not, click on the **'Sign In'** button in the upper right corner and enter your Gmail and its password. Once you are in, click on the button of your Gmail account in the upper right corner, and select **'My Channel'**. You will have the option to create your channel right away, but for your purpose, choose **'Use a Business or Other Name'** from the bottom of the page. Now, enter the name of your brand and then click **'Create'**. Keep in mind that this can be updated later from your settings menu.

Channel Icon and Channel Art

Now that your channel is created, it is time to customize it. Simply select the **'Edit Layout'** and let's get started. The first thing you need to do is to create a channel icon and art. Channel icon and channel art for YouTube are what the profile picture and cover image are for Facebook – they are the first thing that your visitors see and therefore leave the first impression.

Click on the default red picture to add your channel icon. Choose a file from your computer, but keep in mind that this picture will be used on your Grail and Google+ accounts as well. 800 x 800 pixels are recommended here.

Next, click on the **'Add channel art'** button found in the center of your channel and upload your preferred image. Here, 2560 x 1440 pixels are recommended.

Describing Your Brand

After uploading your pictures, it is time to add some details about your business and customize the **'About'** tab. Write a gripping and compelling description that will explain your business briefly and also let people know about the type of videos that will be uploaded on your channel. Make sure to include links to your website and other social media platforms, as well as to include your business email address.

A great option that YouTube provides is the fact that you can customize your channel differently for unsubscribed and subscribed users. The best way to use this option is to add a *channel trailer* that will lure visitors to hit the 'subscribed' button.

The channel trailer is a video description of your channel and it should be short (not longer than 90 seconds; 45 seconds is the best) and appealing. Its main purpose should be to welcome visitors and encourage them to subscribe.

Once you make your channel trailer, it is time to upload it:

1. Make sure that the channel customization is on. You can check this after clicking the settings icon next to 'Subscribe'. Click **'Customize the layout of your channel'** and then hit **'Save'**.

2. Click on the arrow button found in the upper right corner to upload your trailer. Choose the right file from your computer and click on **'For New Users'** once it uploads.

3. Select **'Channel Trailer'**, choose the file you've uploaded, and hit **'Save'**.

Once you get your first 100 subscribers, your channel is more than 30 days old, and you have a channel icon and art uploaded, your YouTube profile will become eligible for a unique and custom URL, which will give it a more professional look.

Appointing the Roles

Before you actually start uploading videos and begin your YouTube marketing strategy, you need to specify how many members of your team will have access to your brand's YouTube channel and what their roles will be.

Once you give them access to the Google account, there are three different role options:

Owner – They will have full power meaning they can add/remove managers, respond/delete comments or reviews, edit information, etc.

Manager – Managers can have all of the editing access as the owner, without the ability to add or remove other managers.

Communications Manager – As the name suggests, the communications manager is mainly in charge of communicating with the audience. They can respond to comments and reviews and do some other editing options, however, they cannot upload new content, view the analytics, or use the video manager.

Go to **'Overview'** ➔ **'Add or remove managers'** and add individuals to manage your YouTube account.

Optimizing for SEO

So, you've successfully created your YouTube business channel. Congratulations! But there is so much more to successful marketing than just creating and uploading engaging videos. For people to watch your videos, they will have to find them first. And how can they do so if you haven't optimized the metadata of your videos?

The metadata of your videos is what gives people information about the video such as its title, category, thumbnail, tags, description, subtitles, etc. and providing the right kind of metadata will help your audience discover your video easily, whether on YouTube or Google search.

Title

When scrolling through the results on YouTube, the first thing that people notice about a video are its title and thumbnail. The title is what hooks the viewer's attention and therefore should be well-thought-out. Conduct a research to understand what it is that people are looking for. Then, include the relevant keywords and important information in the title, but be careful not to go overboard. If your title has more than 60 characters, it will be shown cut-off in the video result pages on YouTube, and people may not even read the whole thing. Keep it simple, clear, and extremely compelling.

Description

Just like your title, the description of the video should also contain relevant keywords that will help potential viewers discover your video easily. But as important as the description is, you need to keep in mind that most people do not actually bother to read it. Unless they are interested, that is. Your job is to make them interested. YouTube usually shows only the first 2-3 lines of the description. If viewers want to read the rest of it, they have to click the 'show more' button for the remaining content. Make sure to polish and re-polish the beginning of the description as much as it takes for it to be compelling so that your viewers would want to read the entire content.

If your description contains CTAs or some important links that you want to share with your audience, make sure to include them in the beginning of the description where people will be able to see them even without clicking 'show more'.

Another thing when it comes to writing the description, it is important to always include a transcript of your video. Why? Because your video itself is filled with keywords. By writing a short transcript with these keywords you will significantly improve your SEO and eventually, your brand's ranking.

Tags

Tags are great because they can associate your brand's videos with other, similar videos on YouTube, which only widens their reach and improves your visibility. For that purpose, make sure that your important keywords are tagged. Highlighting the most relevant keywords first is a crucial part of your brand's SEO optimization so make sure to choose your words wisely.

Category

Once your video is uploaded, you will need to choose the category under which it will be shown on YouTube. You can choose the video's category under **'Advanced settings'**. You can choose from Film & Animation, Travel & Events, Entertainment, Music, Pets & Animals, Educations, Nonprofits & Activism, People & Blogs, Sports, Autos & Vehicles, How-to & Style, Science & Technology, News & Politics, and Comedy.

Choosing your category carefully is very important as the categories are what group your videos with the relevant ones on YouTube. For instance, if you are selling dog shampoo and list your video under People & Blogs instead of Pets & Animals, you may not reach your target audience.

Thumbnail

As mentioned earlier, the thumbnail of your video is extremely important as it is, along with the title, the first thing that people see on YouTube after discovering your video. The thumbnails have a significant impact on the number of views and should be selected carefully. Although YouTube will recommend an option of a few auto-generated thumbnails after uploading, it is highly recommended to skip this option and include a custom thumbnail instead. Choose a shot that will encourage people to click and that represents your video in a good light. YouTube says that 90% of the most successful videos on YouTube actually have custom thumbnails, so you cannot be wrong with this one.

SRT Files

Closed captions and subtitles are extremely helpful for viewers, but that is not the only reason why your video should include them. SRT files are also a great way for you to highlight your keywords. Whether you choose to add a timed subtitles file or a transcript of your text, SRT files are a valuable SEO optimization tool that you should definitely take advantage of.

To add SRT files go to **'Video Manager'** ➔ **'Videos'**. There, choose the video to which you want to add the SRT files and select the drop-down arrow on the right. Select **'Subtitles/CC'** and choose accordingly.

End Screens and Cards

Adding end screens and cards is a valuable option offered by YouTube that can help you encourage your viewers to visit your website, check out your other videos, and even to answer poll questions.

Cards are the small notifications that usually appear in the upper right corner of your video. Your card can contain a poll, a link, another video, or can be used to promote another channel on YouTube. You can add up to 5 cards at the same time, but be careful as too many inquiries have the tendency to put off viewers. If you absolutely must add a few cards, make sure to space them out well so that your viewers can take several actions without feeling overwhelmed.

To add a card go to **'Video Manager'** → **'Cards'** → **'Add Card'** and choose whether you want to create a Link, Video or Playlist, Channel, or a Poll card. After creation, simply drag the card to where you want it to appear on the video.

End Screens are those last seconds of the video that encourage the viewers to take further action such as subscribe to channel, visit a Facebook page, click the like button, check out another video, etc. You can add 5-20 extra seconds to your videos and ask your viewers to engage with your brand.

To add an end screen go to **'Video Manager'**, click on the drop-down arrow then choose **'End Screens and Annotations'**. There, you can choose which elements you want your end screen to include, just keep in mind that it is required to promote another YouTube video or a playlist, so even if you only wanted to encourage viewers to visit your website, you'd have to also encourage people to watch some other video of your brand there.

Playlists

You may think that creating playlists is not worth your time, but this feature is a real gem for the YouTube marketers. Why? Because it increases your visibility. By creating your playlists, you can combine videos not only from your channels but other YouTube channels as well. And the best part is that these playlists are listed and shown separately in the search results. For instance, if you make a collection of your videos and include some popular ones with similar content, you will help other people who may not have heard about your brand before, discover you.

To create a playlist, click on the '+' button under your video, select **'Create new playlist',** choose the name for your playlist, and click on **'Create'**. To add more videos, simply use the same button but instead of clicking on 'Create new playlist' choose the already existing one to feature your videos there.

Making the Videos

Now that your YouTube channel is all set up and know what you have to do in order to optimize it for SEO, the next step is to learn how to make killer videos that people will actually watch. After all, those videos that are of high quality are the most important part of YouTube marketing. Your high-class strategy will not have much value if your videos are not created carefully, addressing the right audience.

So let's start enriching your channel with amazing content, shall we?

Type of YouTube Videos

Before you say "Action" and actually start filming, first you need to determine what the type of your video will be. There are eight types of videos that YouTube marketers usually create:

1. Customer Testimonials

Customer testimonials are something that every successful brand should film at some point and upload to their YouTube channel. They are short interview-like videos where content customers are filmed to express their satisfaction with the product/service, share their positive experience with others, as well as recommend the brand to anyone who is considering their products or services.

2. Explainer Videos

Explainer videos are also called *tutorial videos* or *how-to videos* and their main purpose, as the name suggests, is to explain to customers how to use a particular product or service. They are also a very detailed and thoughtful way to explain some more complex customer support questions.

3. On-Demand Demonstration Videos

Demonstration videos are usually short videos filmed with the purpose to briefly demonstrate the use of a particular product or service, as well as to reveal its benefits to potential customers.

4. Case Studies and Project Reviews

Whether it is the case studies of a successful campaign or the 5-star reviews of a certain product, the purpose of these videos is to recap the positive results and share them with the world in order to turn potential customers into buyers.

5. Thought Leader Interviews

These videos are quality interview with experts of your niche with the sole purpose of increasing the credibility of your brand.

6. Video Blogs

Video blogs or usually called *vlogs* are frequently posted videos (on a daily or weekly basis), documenting some events. Video blogs are popular among the YouTube marketers because they are a great way to get people to visit your website. By summarizing a certain blog post and uploading the video to your YouTube channel, you also give your customers multiple options in which they can absorb your content.

7. YouTube Live

YouTube Live is a feature that allows you to broadcast live to your subscribers. This amazing feature is of extreme value for your marketing strategy because it allows you to connect with your audience live, and lets them engage in real-time discussions.

8. Event Videos

Event videos are those videos that show some experience of a conference, auction, or some other event, and are a great way to share the positive reaction of the present crowd to your online viewers.

The Script of Your Videos

Now that you've chosen the type of your video, it is time to carefully craft its script. Before you start filming, there are a couple of steps that you need to take care of in order to ensure that the video will provide value.

The Goal

Before you turn your idea into reality, you need to determine first what that idea should accomplish. What is the goal of your video? What are you trying to achieve by uploading it to your channel? Do you want to increase the number of subscribers? Enhance your brand's awareness? Drive more traffic to your website?

Of course, you want all those things, but the key to making a successful video that will be watched, is a singular goal. Make each video with a single goal in mind. This will help you stay focused and prevent tackling different things at one time, which is the best marketing practice there is.

Create the Story

Now for the creative part. After determining your goal, it is time to wake up your imagination and craft a good story for your video. This should serve as a blueprint and an outline that will be followed during the shooting process. A good video storyboard should include:

- A frame for each scene

- A short description for each of the scenes

- The lines for each of the scenes

- Camera directions and details for the shooting (for instance, wide shots, tight shots, etc.)

The Extra Elements

If you are planning to include some additional multimedia elements in your videos such as slides or graphics, then you should plan for them in advance. Make sure that the extra content will be placed without any errors and add them to your storyboard.

The Length of the Video

How long will your video be? This is an important factor in the video making process so make sure to determine this as early as possible. Videos under 2 minutes have the highest degree of audience engagement on YouTube, so keep that in mind when deciding on how long it will take for you to deliver the key message.

The Filming Location

Depending on the type and concept of your video, you may need one, two or several filming locations. Finding the perfect shooting spot can be tricky, so you might want to involve your friends and family to help you out with this one. Whatever you choose, remember that for some locations you may need a shooting permit, so take care of this one beforehand to avoid being sued.

Before shooting, visit each of the locations to determine how to adjust the scenery, take care of the lighting, pay attention to the ambient sounds, etc.

Shooting a High-Quality Video

Unless you are a very successful company and can afford to pay a fancy filming crew to take care of the video making process for you, chances are, you will need some pro tips that will help you make high-quality videos that will be watchable. Whether you are using your smartphone or a semi-professional camera for recording, the tips below will help you populate your channel with professional content:

A Tripod Is a Must. The first impression is often the most important one, especially when trying to represent your brand and promote products/services. If your video starts with a shaky camera, no one will watch it, period. When clicking on the video, people are looking to hear the story behind it, not to be distracted by the unprofessional shooting. If your shot is static, buy a decent tripod that will hold your camera steady for a professional look.

Go for Different Angles. A scene that is shot from only one angle is visually boring. To spice things up, shot each scene from a few different angles so you can edit afterward and create one appealing, expensive-like video.

More is More. Make a habit to always shoot more than you need. That will only give you more material to choose from during the editing process and will cost nothing but a bit more time. After all, it is always easy to cut out what you don't need. Going back and re-filming is not only a hassle but sometimes impossible.

Choose the Manual Mode. I've read somewhere that real photographers use only manual mode because they get to tell the camera what they want and there are no inconvenient surprises like with automation. If your camera has that option, go for a full manual mode to get the most out of filming. That way you can easily adjust the focus and shoot a visually-appealing video.

Invest in Your Microphone. If your video includes speaking, then investing in a high-quality microphone is not an option – it is a must. You don't want to sound like you are talking to your viewers from the end of a tunnel. Even if you are using your smartphone for the video making process, you can purchase a mic that can be plugged into your device and further enhance the sound of your video.

Editing Your Video

After filming, it is time to edit the video material and create a compelling video of high quality to upload to your YouTube channel.

Editing Tools. Chances are, your OS already has some editing software that offers basic tools for editing such as correction of color, cutting clips, or adding titles. However, if you want a video with a more professional look, then spending some money on a more advanced software such as Adobe Premier CC or Final Cut Pro X, is highly recommended. If you want to keep things pretty low-budget, YouTube also offers online editing software for that purpose.

Thumbnails. As discussed earlier, video thumbnails are extremely important. The video thumbnail is what potential viewers will see in their video search results, on your YouTube channel, as well as their suggested column on their right when watching similar videos. The most successful YouTube marketers have their own custom-made thumbnails uploaded, so get creative and make one yourself.

Watermarks. Want to further encourage your viewers to hit the 'subscribe' button? Then adding a watermark is a perfect choice. Watermarks are custom-made 'subscribe' buttons that are placed on your videos with the purpose of attracting the viewer's eye and encouraging them to press conveniently and subscribe to your channel while watching your video.

If you want to add a watermark, go to **'Creator Studio' → 'Channel' → 'Branding'**. Press **'Add a Watermark'** and follow the uploading instructions.

Sound Effects. High-quality sound effects are probably the most important factor that makes the difference between a professional-shot video and an amateur one on a low budget. But you don't have to have a giant budget in order to include movie-like music. Now there are many ways to add a quality sound to your videos without draining your budget.

YouTube itself offers a variety of sound effects of high quality to choose for your videos. But if you are not so crazy about that option, then finding royalty-free music online is perhaps your best solution. There are royalty-free sounds that you can actually download for free, but if you want to add a more professional tone to your videos, then think about investing some money and download the right music for your video for a flat price. Royalty-free means that, once you pay for the download, you are free to use the music file any way you see fit, without having to make additional payments, even if your video skyrockets on YouTube.

Marketing the Videos

Now that your video is filmed, beautifully edited, and successfully uploaded to your YouTube channel, the next step is to find the best marketing strategy and get people to actually click on your video and watch it.

In case you haven't noticed, we've already covered a large chunk of YouTube marketing strategies that will help people discover and watch your videos such as: using relevant keywords, using tags, have a rich and compelling description, have the perfect thumbnail image, include descriptive transcripts, use cards and end screens, and combine your videos with popular ones in playlists. All of these, let's call them tricks, will help you boost the organic traffic, get more views, and improve your ranking. But if you have just embarked the YouTube marketing train, it might be pretty hard to stand out and achieve your goals. The initial (and the most important!) strategy for YouTube marketing is knowing how to *spread the word.*

Spreading the word and letting your audience know that you actually have a YouTube channel where they can check out your videos, is the first thing you need to take care of.

Social Media

Have a Facebook or Instagram account? Sharing your videos on other social media platforms is the best way to let your followers there know about your channel and videos and get them to engage. Fortunately, sharing YouTube videos couldn't be easier. To share a video, simply click the **'Share'** button found underneath the video and select the platform where you want to market the video. Another way is to copy the video URL from the address bar while the video is playing, and then paste the link on your social media page.

But keep in mind that sharing the video alone is not a good marketing strategy. You are not sharing a silly cat video with your friends; you need people to watch and engage. When thinking about sharing a video, also think about why you created the video in the first place. Was it a tutorial to simplify the use and answer some customer questions? If so, the best way is to share your video as a response to that questions. Was it a part of some trend or a campaign? If that was the reason, then do not forget the important #hashtags to ensure that your video is a part of a conversation. And if you simply want to spread awareness around your company, then including the link to the video in your 'About' section as well can be quite beneficial.

Website

Your website or blog is the perfect place for you to market your YouTube channel and videos. If you have a website that is up and running, do not forget to include 'Follow' icons to your social media platforms. This includes YouTube as well. This will help your blog's visitors to easily find your channel and click the 'Subscribe' button to stay updated with your video posts as well.

A great strategy is to also create a video that will be posted as an addition to a certain review, case study, or simply your blog post. This works well both ways because it can not only help you market your videos and gain more views on YouTube, but it can also drive organic traffic to your website and other platforms as well.

To post one of your YouTube videos to your website, find the embed code underneath the video, copy it, and paste it where you want it to be featured.

Email

The worst mistake that marketers can make is getting preoccupied with attracting a new audience and forgetting about the customers that they already have. Once your YouTube channel is packed with some videos, it is time to share the news with your existing users/customers. And what better way to do so than with an email list? Send an email newsletter with helpful information and video and encourage your customers to engage with your brand. You don't like the idea of sending your customers links to your videos? How about inviting them to check out a certain website post where your YouTube video has already been embedded?

Collaboration

Sometimes the solution is in someone else's hands. If your brand is in collaboration with another company that also has a YouTube channel, ask them to collaborate together. This will not only be fun and exciting for both companies, but it is the perfect way to join forces and expand your audience. By creating a video or even a playlist together, you may end up getting a lot of their subscribers and vice versa. The important thing to have in mind though, is that your goals are similar and that the collaboration with the other brand aligns with your strategy.

Q&A Websites

Have you ever visited a Q&A site? They are the perfect place to get a solution to your questions from experts and people that have experience in the field of your interest. www.quora.com is the most popular site right now. Take advantage of it. Monitor the kind of questions that people ask and provide solutions with your video content. Who knows? This might turn out to be your best marketing strategy out there.

Engage, Engage, Engage!

Finally, the solution can be pretty simple. Engage with your existing audience and get them to spread their satisfaction and positive experience. Answer their questions, respond to their comments in a timely manner, ask for their honest feedback, and do not forget to thank them for their support. This is the simplest but most easily forgotten task. Make sure to be there for the users so they can be there for you.

Getting a Handle on YouTube Analytics

Investing your time and effort into creating and uploading professional and helpful videos to your YouTube channel cannot possibly be successful if you are not measuring what you've achieved. Keeping a track of your success can help you pinpoint what you are doing wrong, what works best, and what needs to be improved in order to enhance the success and improve your YouTube ranking.

Every YouTube channel has its **YouTube Analytics** that contains reports of the channel's performance for a certain time period. Understanding exactly what those numbers and graphs mean can help you get a clear picture of whether people find your videos attractive or not. Here is a quick tutorial on how to use Analytics to measure success:

Your Goal

If you don't have a clear goal in mind, you cannot possibly expect to measure your success, because you don't have a standard for your measurements. Knowing exactly why you post your video (remember, one goal per video?) will help you imagine where you see your video to be and where it is actually standing. That way you can understand what areas need improvement and whether you should think about investing in paid ads to drive more traffic to your channel.

Now that you have reminded yourself of what how you expect your videos to perform, it is time to check out whether they have delivered or not. The first thing you need to do is open your YouTube Analytics. Just go to www.youtube.com/analytics (be sure you are logged in). Once you enter you should see a performance overview of your videos for the last 28 days. You can adjust the timeframe and filter the results by the key metrics from there.

Watch Time

Watch time is a report that shows you the total number of minutes that your audience spent watching your content, whether in total or by video. This is an extremely important factor because it is what directly impacts the YouTube ranking. If your video has a high watch time, you should expect it to be ranked high in the video search results.

Average View Duration

The average view duration (retention rate) represents the average percentage that your audience watches per view. To put it simply, it is not the same if a person watches the first 10 seconds or finish watching the entire video. The higher this percentage is, the higher are the chances that your audience will watch the video until the end. Cards and end screens can help you improve this numbers, so if you haven't already included them, go back here and take care of that.

Traffic Sources

This report will show you exactly how your viewers are discovering your video content online. Whether it was the YouTube search, YouTube ads, suggested video, or from an external platform (such as your website or Facebook page), this report will show you how most people landed there. This is a very valuable factor as it clearly shows you what marketing strategy works best and where you need to spend some more time and effort.

Demographics

The demographics report will show you a clear picture of what age group watches your videos the most. But that's not all. You can then break down these groups into geography or gender to further understand your audience and see if your YouTube viewers match your already established buyer persona, or if you need to adjust your goals or videos to hit your target audience better.

Engagement Reports

These reports will show you what it is that your audience engages with the most. Here, you can pinpoint the most viewed, shared, promoted, or commented videos. Plus, this report will also show you how your cards and end screens are performing so you can further optimize your videos.

Advertising on YouTube

So you've done everything that you could and yet, the YouTube Analytics' reports aren't as satisfying as you hoped for. Well, I hate to break it to you, but promoting on social media and embedding on your website and crossing your fingers that someone will watch your videos won't cut it. You need to take some serious action and foot the bill for a high YouTube ranking. That means advertising on YouTube.

Types of YouTube Ads

There are three different types of YouTube ads to invest in. Read on to choose the one that fits your needs and budget the most:

TrueView Ads

TrueView Ads are the standards and most common ads that you see on YouTube videos. You pay for TrueView ads only when the viewer watches at least 30 seconds of the ad, or if they engage with it, for instance, with clicking on a call-to-action. These ads are skippable, which means that if the viewer is not interested in watching them, they can hit the **'Skip'** button on the right, choose not to watch the ad, and you will not pay a dime for that. These skippable ads can be anywhere from 12 seconds to 6 minutes long.

There are two parts of skippable TrueView ads:

#1: Video Discovery Ads

Video Discovery, or previously called In-Display Ads, are those ads that show on the video search result pages, YouTube homepage, and as videos that are related. Once the viewer clicks to watch the video, on the right, a display ad banner will appear.

#2: In-Stream Ads

In-Stream ads are those advertisements that appear within the video and play before the viewer even get the chance to watches the selected video. Usually, viewers have the chance to skip the ad after 5 seconds of playing, if they are not interested. These ads are great for marketers because they can be easily customized with the chance of including different call-to-action buttons.

Preroll Ads

Although technically they are non-skippable in-stream ads, the preroll ads are those ads that the viewers cannot skip, and that appear before, after, or even mid-roll videos. These preroll ads can be from 15-20 seconds long and are most successful if they are created with CTAs in order to optimize the viewer's attention that you have for these limited seconds. Your job here is to create a compelling ad that will encourage the viewers to click on the ad in order to receive something in return (like signing up for a demo product or some event).

Bumpers

The shortest type of ads on YouTube is called bumpers. They are only 6 seconds short and, to be honest, are not the best way to tell a story, however, if you are looking for a quick way to complement the launch of your new product or event, they can be of great value. Make sure to use these few seconds wisely and make sure to include only the elements that you want your viewers to actually remember.

Creating Your Ad Campaign

Once your marketing video is completed, the next step is to create the campaign in which you will advertise your clip on YouTube. To get started, go to Google AdWords account (sign up if you don't have one) and let's create the campaign:

Type – Click on the **'+ Campaign'** button and choose **'Video'** to choose the type of your campaign.

Name – Here, enter the name of your campaign.

Ad Format – Choose the format of your video ad. For instance, choose **'In-stream or video discovery ads'**.

Budget – Set how much money you wish to spend per day. Here, you can also select the method of delivery, meaning you can choose whether to show your video ads evenly during that day (standard delivery), or you can choose to drive views quickly (accelerated delivery).

Networks – You can choose where you want your video ads to appear. You have two options:

1. YouTube Videos: These ads will play before or mid-roll videos.

2. YouTube Search: Your ad will appear on the YouTube homepage, the video search results, and listed in the related video column.

Make sure to create different campaigns for these two networks so you can measure the success separately and more effectively.

Locations – Filter the location of the users that you want the ad to be shown to, for instance, you can only choose California, United States. You also have the option to exclude some places as well.

Language, Device & Mobile Bidding – This is a great option that allows you to specify the device, mobile carrier, and operating system for a more successful targeting. You can also decrease or increase your bid if the video is shown on a mobile device.

Advanced Settings – In this section, you can set the start and end date of your campaign, limit the daily views, create a schedule for when the ad should be displayed, etc. This allows you to personalize your ad and get the most return.

Creating the Video Ad Creative – Once you name your ad group, you can also add the link to the YouTube video that you wish the ad to play for. Then, you will choose whether you wish to display the ad as an in-display or in-stream ad.

Bidding – Choose the maximum price that you want to pay for each ad view.

Targeting – Define your audience even further to ensure views from people who will want to be engaged with the ad. You can target by age, gender, location, interest, parental status, etc.

Advanced Targeting – Here, you can target your audience by relevant keywords or even websites that you want your ad to be shown.

Linking – Finally, if you haven't done it already, link your Google AdWord account to your YouTube channel, Click **'Finish'** and start your campaign.

Instagram

If you still think of Instagram as the social media platform where you post your selfies and well-plated restaurant foods, you need to change your opinion at this instant. Okay, I admit, that's what Instagram was when it first started in October 2010. But fast forward 8 and a half years later, and you see a platform that is filled with valuable tools for businesses. If you want to market your brand successfully online, then having a strong Instagram presence is definitely a must.

Instagram has over 800 million active monthly users, but statistics aside, the main reason why you should choose to learn this platform inside out and decide to have a marketing presence there, is the fact that Instagram users are not just active, they are engaged.

Instagram is all about the visual, and if you happen to be in the ecommerce business, well, marketing your brand on Instagram may just mean hitting the jackpot.

Setting Up Your Instagram Business Account

In order for you to set up your Instagram business page, you first need to have an Instagram account up and running. To do so, you will have to have the Instagram app downloaded.

When you open the app, you will see two options: to log in with Facebook, or to sign up with an Email or Phone. Make sure to use a business email for this purpose to make sure that your Instagram profile will not be linked to your personal Facebook account.

After that, enter your details. Under **Full Name**, enter the name of your business, and under **Username**, write down the unique name for your Instagram profile that will be recognizable so that people can easily find it and engage with the content.

Next, add a profile picture for your Instagram profile. Whether a logo or a photo of your store, the main point is for the picture to be clear and distinctive.

Now that you have an Instagram account, the next step is to make it a business one. In order for your account to be a business account, it will have to be linked with a Facebook business page. Assuming that you have already taken care of that, open your Instagram profile. Tap on the **'Settings'** icon in the upper right corner. Once there, go to **'Switch to Business Profile'** → **'Continue'** to connect with your Facebook page. Keep in mind that your profile will need to be set to public, so make sure that the 'Private' option is not selected.

There, you should see your Facebook page as an option. Select it and click on **'Continue As'.** Tap **'Next'**.

Once you're all set, you will be prompted to enter some company info such as address, phone number, and email address. This is important for your customers to get in touch with you, so make sure to enter valid information. Click **'Done'** and that's it.

Optimizing Your Profile

Congratulations! Now you are a proud owner of an Instagram business account. But wait before thinking you've got what it takes to jump straight to posting your content. There are a couple more steps that need to be taken care of in order for your profile to look professional and, most importantly, attractive to your audience.

As mentioned before, Instagram is all about the visual. That means that it should be a good reflection of your brand, but at the same time, it should also provide a constant aesthetic look.

The Color Scheme

Your Instagram color scheme should be consistent and have a sort of a flow. The colors should go together seamlessly and it should give away a good feeling, whatever you go for the dark and cold or the bright and warm feed.

The Lighting

Just as the color, the lighting is also a crucial element for the aesthetic. If not sure what I mean, think about your favorite magazine for a second. Whatever the subject there, the good lighting is what keeps everything together and provides an elegant look.

Evenly Spaced-Out Content

To keep your Instagram profile visually appealing, besides lighting and coloring, the way your photos are spaced out is also an important ingredient. The main thing is that your feed should blend together. Try not to clump together a lot of busy photos, but find a balance between them and the minimal ones for a beautiful and attractive look.

Have Consistent Editing

Another important thing you need to have in mind before you actually start uploading the photos, is that they need to have a consistent editing style. You don't need to use only one filter, of course, but try to have a more cohesive look by keeping the style the same so that your photos will flow.

Writing Your Bio

The Instagram bio is by far the most under-utilized part of Instagram profiles, but that doesn't mean that it's not important. Quite the opposite, actually. If you are a business that wants to promote its products or services on Instagram, then having an eye-catching bio that will introduce your brand to customers is so much more than just an option.

But simply writing your name, website, and address will not do the trick. You will need to actually write down what your business is and what you do in a shortly descriptive and equally creative way. This is the time to stand out and let people know what makes your brand better than other similar ones. If you have a certain tool or service that makes you stand out, include that in your info.

Another thing you need to include in your bio is *#hashtags.* Thanks to an update that happened in 2018, your profile username and hashtags from your bio are now clickable links. By including '#' and '@' before the words, they will become a hyperlink that will take your audience to another page. Pretty beneficial for promoting your brand, right?

Once you've set everything up, take one final look and see if you're satisfied with the way you have introduced your brand to the world.

Types of Insta Posts

If all looks good, it's time to post your content on Instagram. But before you do that, let's take a look at the different types of posts that you can share on your Instagram profile:

Images

The most popular type of post on Instagram is the image post. Keep in mind that when posting your brand's images on Instagram, it is important to share a variety of them. That way you will show your bra--nd's diversity and also help your audience engage with your content in many ways.

Another thing you need to understand when posting images, is that your audience (especially Instagram audience) is looking for genuine photos, not sales pitches and advertisements. Then how to promote your products, you may think. Try to focus on delivering a real-life message, not on sharing product images only. For instance, if you are selling clothes, instead of taking a photo of your newest shirt, try to post a photo of a model wearing that shirt with beautiful scenery in the background.

Behind-the-Scenes Posts

This is probably the type of post that is appreciated the most. Posting from behind the scenes allows your audience to take a look at how things are done in your company and get a feel of the atmosphere there. For instance, you can share a photo that will show your employees at work on a busy day.

The key to these posts is realness. The post needs to look authentic and not staged in order to attract your customer's eye.

Reposts from Employees

Looking for an original way to post? How about reposting some great content that your employees have already shared? Reposting images from the Instagram profiles of your employees (and tagging them, of course) is a great way to make your brand seem a bit more 'human' and enhance the originality of your profile. This way you will show your audience that your team has a special bond, which will encourage them to engage.

Motivational Posts

Motivational posts include simple images with a quote or other uplifting and motivational text. But as much as these posts can help you increase the value of your brand, if not executed tastefully, they will sound cheesy and fake. Taste them sparingly to look more original.

Influencer Posts

Influencer posts are those posts that are shared by a celebrity or another well-known person who has a massive fan base. For instance, if you sell healthy and organic drinks, you may want to choose to contact an athlete or a famous wellness coach to post a picture of them drinking one of your smoothies. The point here is to extend your audience and reach some of the influencer's fans. How to do it? Find and contact an influencer with the inquiry, offering something in return. Many of them will do it for free samples, but others may ask money in return.

Educational Posts

Those posts that offer quick tips on how to make or do something are called educational posts. They can either be videos or photos, but the main thing is that they offer simple instructions that the audience can follow in order to achieve something.

User-Generated Content

If reposts from employees meant sharing images and videos that your employees have posted, user-generated content means curating posts that have been shared by your followers. Deciding to share a post from a customer will not only make their day, but it will also show your other followers that you truly care for your customers. Just make sure to credit the original image or video and tag the poster.

Newsjacking

Newsjacking means trending holiday posts. But I do not only mean the huge holidays such as Christmas or Valentine's Day. There is a holiday for pretty much everything, so you might want to consider getting into its spirit and share upbeat messages for these carefree moments.

TAKING QUALITY IMAGES

Now that you've learned what kind of images you can share on Instagram, let's see how to actually post appealing ones that will draw the attention of your audience and make them hit the 'like' button and comment.

First of all, follow the rules for the image size:

Square Images – 1080 x 1080 pixels

Landscape Images – 1080 x 566 pixels

Profile Images – 1350 x 1080 pixels

The Rule of Thirds

Moving the subject from the center and creating an imbalance of the photo is a very popular and appealing technique that most photographers love to use. Called the rule of the thirds, this technique will be loved by your followers.

For convenient photo taking, make sure that the grid lines on your smartphone are turned on.

Single Subject Is the Key

Posting chaotic photos will not catch your follower's eye, as simple and organized ones will. Try to focus on a single subject when shooting photos. That means cropping out and getting rid of unnecessary things in the frame, making the extra subject blurry, or shooting against a simple and clear background.

Say Yes to the Negative Space

Negative space is a term for the empty space that is around your subject. In terms of promoting a single product, shooting with a lot of negative space is just the thing you need. That way, your follower's eye will be drawn right where you want it to be – on your product.

Take Advantage of Different Perspective

We people see the world around us from an eye level. For that purpose, professional photographers, usually, take photos from a different perspective and use various angles, to make the image seem as realistic as possible.

Play with Patterns and Symmetry

Whether a wooden table or a tiled floor, choose an attractive pattern that will be disrupted by your subject. Try to break the rule of thirds from time to time, and add some symmetry to your photos by placing your subject in the middle of your chosen pattern.

Natural Light is Your Friend

Natural light works best in photography. Try not to overshadow your subject by standing overhead your lighting, but tend to take advantage of the natural light by shooting outdoors or next to a window.

Videos

As long as the video is 60 seconds or less long, it can be uploaded on Instagram.

Boomerangs

Boomerang is an Instagram setting that allows you to take 3-second videos that can play both, forwards and backwards. By tapping the camera icon on Instagram and choosing the **'Boomerang'** setting, you can easily upload a Boomerang to Instagram.

Boomerangs are a fun way to showcase upbeat circumstances such as jumping or high-fiving.

You can also create a Boomerang by combining photos for a repetitive and entertaining video.

Hyperlapse

Hyperlapse for Instagram is a tool that will allow you to cut your long videos short and transform them into content that can be posted on Instagram. Download the app Hyperlapse and you can record your own time lapse videos, save, and upload.

Instagram Live

Just like Facebook Live, Instagram also offers the option to share live content. If you are interested in engaging with your customers this way, just open your Instagram camera, choose the **'Live'** setting, and then simply hit the **'Start Live Video'** button. Once you start your live video stream, all of your followers who are online at the moment, will receive a notification. Your live audience can also engage real-time by commenting on your live video, which is a great opportunity for a real-time Q&A session with your customers.

IGTV

IGTV or Instagram TV is the most recent video feature by Instagram. This is a way for Instagram users to watch longer vertical videos, which can also be great for your marketing strategy if you were thinking about including some longer explainer videos or even some interviews.

IGTV can be accessed either through the Instagram app, or through its own IGTV app that can be downloaded from your App Store. If you are thinking about posting on IGTV though, you will have to download the app and create a channel there. After that, you can upload videos that are anywhere from 15 seconds to 10 minutes in length. If you have a verified account you can run your videos for up to an hour. You can only use IGTV on your smartphone, as this platform cannot be accessed through your desktop computer yet.

Keep in mind that this is not the same as Instagram Live. IGTV is previously recorded and uploaded footage, which gives you the opportunity to fine-tune and edit your video for as long as you'd like.

Instagram Stories

Instagram stories is a very popular feature on Instagram that is basically, a solution to over-posting. It is basically a way for you to post on Instagram frequently, but without polluting your main feed.

This is a time-sensitive feature that shows a bit rawer look, unlike your filtered photos. It is much more authentic than your usual posts, which is why it is deeply appreciated by the followers.

There are three ways in which you can post your Instagram Story:

1. Tap the camera icon in the top left corner

2. Type the **'Your Story +'** found above your feed

3. Or simply swipe right with your finger to open your camera

Your story can also be filtered or doodled on. You can also add text or even include a GIF, music, add a location, and a ton of other fun features. And the best part? Instagram actually allows you to tag another Instagram account in your Story, so that is a cool way to connect with a similar business, a team member, or you can also use this feature to personally tag a customer to thank for the support.

To publish, just press the **'Your Story +'** button, or you can simply choose to save for later and post the story when it is more convenient for you. You can find your story at the top of your main feed and also through your profile picture.

Writing Eye-Catching Captions

Although it is the picture that first catches the viewer's eye, if the caption underneath it is less than remarkable, your audience will not be tempted to engage with it. But how to write outstanding captions? Follow these simple tips below to avoid getting overwhelmed with finding the right words.

Take Your Time

Okay, you are not writing a chapter for your novel. You don't actually need days to brainstorm the perfect line that will accompany your new picture, but writing a couple of drafts and asking the opinion of your friends and family can surely help. The main purpose of your posts is to be engaging to users, especially with the new Instagram algorithm. When users visit the Instagram app, the top posts that they see are the ones that Instagram thinks they will find to be the most engaging. That should be a good reason for you to find the time to craft captions that will wow your audience.

The Beginning Counts the Most

Instagram allows 2,200 characters in the captions, which is a great thing if you are comparing this platform with Twitter where you cannot post more than 140 characters. However, keep in mind that your audience will not see the whole text on their screens. It is only the first couple of lines that are shown; to read the rest of the text, your audience needs to click the 'More' button. If you really want to tell a story that people will actually read, make the first few lines as attention-grabbing as possible, to get your customers hooked. There is no reason for you to shy away from getting into details and writing longer captions, as long as you write killer beginnings. However, if you want your audience to do most of the talking, then shorter captions work best.

Engage!

It seems I cannot stress this enough, but ENGAGEMENT really is the key to successful marketing. Otherwise, you are just another brand selling unimportant stuff to people. To encourage your audience to engage, make sure to <u>always</u> include a call-to-action in your captions and ask your audience to like, share, and comment on your post.

Work on Your Instagram Voice

Remember how we said that you need to have a separate approach for every platform? Your voice should be different for each of your social media profiles. What promotes your brand on LinkedIn will probably not work for Instagram. Your posts on Instagram should be carefree, upbeat, and written with a unique tone that will become recognizable for your brand over time. Give your brand a distinct feel by playing with words, colors, emojis, and other creative tools.

Their Majesty, the #Hashtags

Unless you are new to social media and not that present on the internet, then you probably already know what hashtags are. They are the keyword phrases that are spelled together, without spaces, and have the '#' sign standing proudly before them. Although they were born on Twitter, hashtags have now completely taken over social media.

Why should you use hashtags? Because they will help your content get noticed, and when you take into consideration that Instagram has over 80 million photos shared every day, you see how that's useful, right? Get it right, and your audience will engage in no time.

There are three ways in which your audience can see tagged content on Instagram:

1. First, they see their TOP 9 posts, which are tagged posts that Instagram thinks the user will most likely want to engage with

2. The most RECENT 9 posts, which shows tagged posts displayed in chronological order

3. RELATED hashtags, which displays similar hashtags that people use to discuss that or a related topic.

To make sure that you can broaden the reach of your post, use a few extra hashtags that are related and that will help your audience notice the photo. For instance, if you want to tag your photo with #smoothie, you may want to add hashtags like #vegan, #healthysnack, or #matchapowder. The point is to tag a few extra details that will explain the subject of your photo.

Note: Your account must be PUBLIC in order for your tagged posts to be displayed on the hashtag feeds.

Finding the Right Hashtag

But what if you cannot decide on which hashtags to use? That can also be easily solved, as finding hashtags within the Instagram app is actually the simplest way. Have a hashtag in mind? Just type your preferred hashtag into the 'Search Bar' of Instagram, filter your search results by Tags, and see how many posts have actually used that hashtag, see related hashtags, and brainstorm some relevant keyword phrases.

Want to increase your reach? Why not throw some trending hashtags into your post and combine them with your specific keywords to make the post more relevant?

Formatting Your Hashtag

Now that you've found the perfect hashtags for your post, you need to decide how to actually use them. The main rule here is to be natural. The used hashtags should have a flow and go well together. Read your post out loud before pressing 'Share' and see how it feels. Sounds kind of spammy? Don't worry! Even if your hashtags cannot be incorporated into the post as you want them to, you can always choose to place them at the end of your post, or even in the beginning. They'll do the same job regardless of their place.

Note: Businesses use an average of 2.5 hashtags per post. Try to limit your hashtags and never include more than 4, to avoid seeming like you try too hard in order to keep your audience interested.

Marketing Your Brand

The biggest mistake you can possibly make is to approach Instagram without a decent marketing strategy in mind. Posting high-quality content with the perfect hashtags will not be enough if you don't have a perfectly crafted strategy. Being a unique social media platform, Instagram requires its own distinctive way of promoting. Read on to see what you can do to help your brand grow with this platform.

Know Your Audience

Knowing exactly who your audience is, is the only way to ensure that you are promoting your brand to the right people and expect engagement in return. If you are already marketing your products on other social media platform, you can use that audience, but keep in mind that Instagram audience is a bit different.

To find your perfect Instagram audience, spend some time monitoring the hashtags that are related to your brand and the products/services you are selling. Check out the people who are using these hashtags, and take a look at their profiles. Take notes of the factors that define your perfect buyer persona and create your perfect audience.

Analyze!

You are just starting out your Instagram marketing journey, which means that you cannot be exactly sure what works and what is not s appreciated by the audience. To get a clear picture of what posts get the highest engagement and what photos sit forgotten, spend some time peeking into your competitors' profiles. See their performance and take notes of the things that have managed to engage the audience the most. After all, wasn't it Picasso who said that great artists steal? I am not talking about copyright infringement, of course, but use their profiles as a guidance of what and when to share to connect with your followers.

Post When Your Audience is Active the Most

If you type "what is the best time to post on Instagram" on Google, you will find a number of websites all showing recent statistics based on millions of posts and user engagement. In fact, the most recent ones say that the best time to share your content is between 9 and 11 am EST. But that does not mean that that's the time when YOUR brand's audience is most active.

There are many ways in which you can find the perfect time to post for your business. Monitoring your audience and taking notes on when different time zones are the most active, as well as tracking your posts' progress over time are both great gauges. But, if you are looking for the most hassle-free option, then downloading some algorithms that will automatically calculate this for you is probably the best choice.

If you don't like any of these options, then sticking to the rule of 9am-11am can also be productive. Also, consider other factors that are important for your business as well. For instance, if your audience is made of teenagers and young adults, then avoid posting early in the morning.

Schedule Your Posts

Once you find out what the perfect time for posting is for your business, make sure to actually share your posts then. The best way to ensure that the post will not slip your mind and will actually be shared at the right time, is to schedule it.

Simply, write down your post and open the drop-down menu found at the bottom of your screen. There, choose **'Publish on Scheduled Date'**, select the preferred date and time, and wait for Instagram to take care of the rest for you. If you are too busy, you can also use a scheduling tool for this purpose where you can write a couple of posts in advance and schedule the date and time when you want them to be published. www.sendible.com and www.later.com both include great management tools for your Instagram profile.

Be Consistent!

Although we have already mentioned this, consistency really is the key. In order for it to be successful, your brand first needs to be consistent on Instagram. And I do not mean only with the posts. Consistency should run all over your feed, from the colors of your profile to how your photos are organized. Knowing what your brand's personality is and adjusting your content to match it, is the best way to catch some eyes and attract new followers.

Attracting Followers

Although every single one of the previously mentioned techniques will help you attract followers on Instagram, there are a couple of tricks that you need to have up your sleeve in order to increase your fan base and get some more likes.

Become a Follower

Assuming that your name and bio are written in a compelling manner, that your profile is optimized as discussed before, and that you've already started posting quality content, the next thing you need to do is start following accounts. Following similar accounts and some other interests that are related to your business will help you become a part of a community that might throw many followers your way. Once you start following people and businesses, Instagram will also suggest other related accounts that you can become a fan of.

But don't let that end there. When you become their follower, start interacting with their content. That will not only spread awareness of your brand, but it will also humanize it, which people greatly appreciate.

Ask for Interaction

Asking people to spread the word is a great marketing strategy that might require some more work, but always pays out. Start with your friends and family and get them to share your account and ask their followers to become your followers. Get in touch with brand ambassadors and kindly ask them to share the content you post with other similar accounts that might help you increase your follower list. Just try not to be pushy and always give something in return. Free samples and generous discounts always seem to do the trick.

Partnering up with an influencer can be pretty valuable. By having the influencer promoting your products, you can 'borrow' some of their followers and drive more traffic to your account.

Go with Instagram Stories

Take advantage of Instagram Stories for more exposure of your brand. How? Besides being a great tool that will help you connect your already existing audience, Instagram Stories can also increase your list of followers, thanks to the fact that they appear on the Instagram Search page. That means that even if someone is not your follower, they can still find your Instagram Stories from the Explore page when searching for something similar.

Promote

Just like with Facebook and YouTube, promoting your Instagram profile on your website and other social media platforms, is the simplest, but sometimes the easiest way to attract new followers that will become your fans on Instagram.

Turning Followers into Customers

Having a lot of Instagram followers can be great for your business. But if those people simply click the 'Follow' button and your connection with them ends there, then your marketing strategy will, most likely, go up in smoke. The key isn't to gather as many followers as possible but to actually turn them into customers. Here are some things that can help you encourage your followers to take some action:

Promotions. People on Instagram love promotions and first-time sales. Limited deals and special offerings can attract your followers to give your brand a chance and see what you are selling. Just remember to emphasize the importance of fast action and mention a fixed deadline so your followers can take the plunge as soon as possible.

Charity. Looking for a way to attract more millennials? How about setting aside some of your profit and donating it to a charity? Studies show that more than 80 % of the millennials expect companies to make generous donations, so try to live up to their expectations. Besides building compassion for your brand, that way you can also get your followers to get involved and support a really important cause. That might turn them into long-term customers of yours.

Contests. Contests are the perfect way to get people to try out your products. Make it a requirement for people to follow your account or even make a post by tagging your brand in order to enter the contest.

Teasers. Posting teasers of your new products is the perfect way to let your audience have a quick look at what you are working on. Combine your teasers with limited promotions and let people purchase your hot, new product for a special price.

Live Launches. Instagram Live offers a great opportunity for you to launch your new products live. This will encourage your customers to get engaged, since this option offers a chance for them to ask you some questions about the product in real time.

What About Analytics?

I hate to disappoint you, but Instagram doesn't have an analytics tool like the built-in ones that Facebook and YouTube offer. Fingers crossed, this will soon be changed for the better. However, that doesn't mean that you cannot track your Instagram success. Below you will find some tips that will help you measure your brand's growth on Instagram and get a clear picture of your business' performance.

First of all, once you switch to a Business account, Instagram does offer some limited tools such as measuring the growth of your followers, their engagement, the organic reach, etc. You can access this tool by clicking on the **'View Insights'** button that's found just below your photos and videos.

If you are looking for a more in-depth way to track your Instagram metrics, then purchasing a third-party tool that will allow you to measure your performance more effectively is probably a good choice. https://pro.iconosquare.com/ is a great management tool for that purpose. Their pricing varies from 29 euros to 79 euros per month, depending on your plan and commitment, but the best part is that they offer a 14-day free trial for you to see what they can do for your marketing strategy and decide whether they are worth the investment.

You can also go to your Facebook's Ad Manager for some Instagram metrics, but keep in mind that this option is pretty limited and it is not for every post or campaign.

Advertising on Instagram

Once you become active on Instagram, you need to consider investing in advertising your content there in order to increase your traffic and get more shares. If you are familiar with Facebook advertising then you have already halfway through Instagram marketing, as the setup and budgeting for your Insta ads are actually done through Facebook.

To begin the process, your Instagram Business account must be claimed and linked to your Facebook Page.

Once you take care of that, choose your editor of choice (Ads Manager, Facebook Ads API or Power Editor). The Ads Manager is the most popular with social media marketers, so you might want to choose that tool.

The next step is selecting the objective for your ad. You will see that there are quite a few options, but for Instagram advertising, these are the ones that you need to choose from:

- Brand Awareness

- Engagement

- Reach

- Traffic

- Conversions

- App Installs

- Video Views

Then, name your ad set, and target your audience. You will be given a few factors to set, such as age, location, gender, behavior, work, etc. Or, if you have one, you can also choose a previously-created custom audience.

Then, choose the **'Edit Placement'** option and click on **'Instagram'** under the given platforms. This is a very important step because if you do not choose Instagram, you will only advertise on Facebook.

Next, you will be asked to set your budget and schedule your ads. As discussed earlier, complete this step and move forward to setting up your content. There are two options for you here, you can either choose to boost an existing post, or you can upload a new photo or video to run as an advertisement.

Once everything is set, simply click on the **'Place Order'** button and that's it. Your Instagram ad campaign is ready to run. Just be sure to report on your performance and keep a track of the ad progress. You can find the metrics for this purpose either in the Facebook Ads Manager or in your marketing software, in case you are using one.

Twitter

With approximately 6,000 new tweets per second, Twitter is definitely a great platform for your business. Whatever your goals may be, chances are, a huge chunk of the 326 million of monthly active Twitter users represent your target audience. With that in mind, it is safe to say that marketing your brand on Twitter can turn out to be a very profitable strategy for you. But simply signing up and tweeting will not be enough. Just like with any other social media platform, you also need a well-crafted marketing strategy for Twitter. This chapter will help you learn how to promote your brand on Twitter and discover the possibilities hiding behind Larry the bird.

How is Twitter Different?

We already talked about the importance of having a different approach to your social media channels. What works for Facebook may not work for your Twitter profile. But when it comes to social media platforms, Twitter really is the one that stands out.

Unlike Instagram or Pinterest, Twitter does not put the emphasis on broadcasting content. Instead, Twitter is all about the conversation and communication between users, whether ordinary people, companies or even government officials.

The top reasons why businesses mostly use Twitter are:

- Sharing information

- Branding

- Driving engagement

- Interacting with customers

- Reputation management

- Networking

Twitter is the platform that thrives off the interaction. That's how it is different. Because it is not a platform that has consumption and distribution of content as a main purpose. On Twitter, people usually go to become a part of an interaction and engage with the content, not to watch videos or scroll through photos.

Creating Your Twitter Profile

If you're just a person who's interested in what the world's leaders have to say next, sure, you can just sign up, upload a photo (or not), and start retweeting. But if you are a business and want to market your brand on Twitter, then an in-depth and carefully-created profile is indeed required.

Follow these next few steps to create a Twitter account for your business:

1. Go to www.twitter.com.

2. Click on the **'Sign Up'** button.

3. Enter the required information and then hit **'Create my account'.**

4. When you click **'Next'** on your homepage, Twitter will ask you to follow 5 people. Make sure that they are related to your business in some way.

5. You can choose to add contacts from your email address at this point, but this step is optional. Your Twitter account is now created.

Go to your profile and click on **'Edit Profile'**. The first thing you need to do is upload your profile picture, which for business is usually their logo or some other photo that represent their brand.

The Bio

Unfortunately, you only get 160 characters to introduce your business to the Twitter world. On the plus side, this gives you an opportunity to get really creative, carefully select your words, and say only the things that matter the most.

Just like on Facebook, YouTube, and Instagram, your brand's bio on Twitter should also include relevant keywords that will help your customer discover you better. Keep in mind that it should be enticing, upbeat and attract followers. It seems that fun bios work like a magnet for the audience, so you might want to add a humorous line to catch some more eyes.

The Optimization

Your bio is important, but if your whole profile is not strategically optimized, then humorous lines and relevant keywords will not do the trick. Your profile should be able not only to visually attract potential customers, but also to encourage them to actually start a conversation about the products or services that you are selling.

Add a professional profile picture that represents your brand (like your logo or a storefront) and upload a high-quality header image that will complement the profile picture; think an upcoming event or the newest product.

Once your exterior is pleasant to the eye, take advantage of hashtags and emojis, and make sure to post content that your audience will find valuable.

The Verification

Getting verified on Twitter is an important part. A verified profile means that you are the real deal and that your audience can trust you. Having the blue checkmark next to your account name can be of great value for your business, so make sure that you verify your profile right from the start.

Let People Know

Know that your profile is not only up and running, but optimized for success as well, it is time to show it off. Whether on your website, other social media platforms, email signature, or added on the front window of your store, letting people know about your Twitter handle is the best strategy for boosting your list of followers.

The Right Marketing Strategy

Marketing your brand on Twitter goes way beyond setting up your profile the right way. It is the proper mix of activities that will boost the process of promoting your brand, and in turn, bring you more customers. But to do so, these marketing-oriented activities must be planned for and carefully designed. Here is how you can power-pack the process of marketing your brand on Twitter:

Listen and Take Notes

When people think of marketing (whether on social media or not), they usually have investing money in mind. And while it is true that the more you invest, the higher the chances for returns, when it comes to promoting your brand, the crucial strategy is often glossed over. The first step, before reaching for your wallet, is to see exactly where you (and your competition) stand. And since we are talking about Twitter marketing, the first step is to check just how engaged are people with your brand.

The very first thing you need to tackle, is to check what the community on Twitter is talking about your brand. What are people interested in the most? What do they think you should improve? What are they not satisfied with? Knowing this can help you crush the competitors and get instant feedback from your customers.

Here are some things that you need to listen for on Twitter:

- The name of your brand

- The name of your products and services

- Your competition

- Your brand's slogans

- Some buzzword in your industry

- The name of your CEO or some other representatives

- Campaign names

- Other important keywords

Take notes of the things that are relevant for your brand and incorporate in your other marketing activities in order to have more satisfied customers.

Create Great Content

This goes without saying, but posting great content is usually what hooks the audience, makes them retweet, share, and engage with your brand. You have only 280 characters, so you should be picky with your words, and say only the things that are the most relevant for your brand and that are highly likely to resonate with your Twitter audience.

Be Helpful. Besides listening to what they have to say or engaging with them directly, it is great to actually show your audience that you care about their needs and interests by helping them in some way. Sharing a trending content that your audience will find helpful is a great way to become more appreciated by your customers. If you don't know how to find one, visit download the *'TrendSpottr'* app and discover some emerging trends.

Use #Hashtags. Ok, I've said this too many times, but hashtags are the single most important thing when it comes to Twitter marketing. Without them, you may as well be writing in your notebook, not sharing your content online. Why? Because it is the hashtags that make sure that your content will be actually discovered and seen by people.

Be Conversational. Making Twitter one-dimensional is a social-media marketing crime. Your Tweets shouldn't be sole broadcasts, but have to open the door for interaction and conversation:

- Ask your audience questions

- Make sure that at least 30 percent of your Tweets are replies

- Do not Tweet mere links; make sure to include a line of your own thoughts, as well

- Make sure to Tweet out directly to your audience

Plan Ahead

You should always be active. That means that for every holiday and special event, you need to get into the spirit. When late November rolls around, you should start with your Christmas tweets. Come mid-January, your Valentine's tweets need to be decorating your Twitter profile. Be in touch with the latest trends, and do not forget to use the right #Holiday hashtags.

Post at the Right Time

Tweets do not last forever. Just because you talked about something ten days ago, does not mean that, when your audience decides that it is time to address the issue, they will engage with your content. It is important to know what the right time to post is in order to be in the middle of the conversation.

Tweet Regularly. Tweeting once a day is a great way to stay active and participate in the hottest conversations. You can try to post more than that, but keep your eyes open and see how that will affect your Twitter presence. That way, you can find the frequency that works best for your brand.

Stick to the Best Practice. It is said that the best times to post on Twitter are 12 pm, 5 pm, and 6 pm. Of course, this depends on your audience, so experimenting and measuring here is, again, recommended in order to find what suits you the most.

Schedule Your Tweets. Once you determine the best times to share your content, schedule your Tweets to ensure that you will get the most engagement for each of your Tweets. https://hootsuite.com/ is a great tool that can help you with scheduling your Tweets.

Twitter Video

Although Twitter is not the first thing that comes to mind when thinking about promoting your brand through video content, statistics say that the Twitter community is very much interested in digesting videos, as well.

There are a few options available when it comes to sharing videos via Twitter:7

1. First, you can use the native feature on Twitter that allows you to record up to 140 seconds and upload directly.

2. Another option is to use a live streaming app called Periscope (owned by Twitter) which integrates into your profile and makes sure that your live stream will be seen by your followers. Once you are done recording, the stream will become available to your audience.

Thread Tweets Together

Want to provide content in an even more organized matter? Try threading tweets together. This facility allows you to start a tweet and then continue adding more tweets to the original one, by simply threading them to the first tweet. This is a great way to tell a story or keep an ongoing conversation alive, without having content all over the place.

Measuring the Results

Measuring what your marketing strategy has achieved so far is the best way to evaluate your Twitter success and determine just how much your audience is engaged with your brand. This simple activity can help you pinpoint your weak spots, as well as your strengths, and help you determine how you should change the strategy and what is worth investing in.

Twitter Analytics

Twitter Analytics is the built-in tool for tracking the overall performance of your Twitter account. To use Twitter Analytics, click on your avatar and then select the **'Analytics'** in order to see your month-by-month highlights. You can also jump straight to analytics.twitter.com.

There you will find:

Top Tweet – The tweet that has earned the most impressions for a selected month.

New Followers – The number of people that have clicked the 'Follow' button for the given month.

Top Follower – This represents the person who has the most followers (out of your New Followers).

Top Mention – A tweet where a user mentions your brand that has earned the most impressions for that month.

Engagements – Anything that users click on (photos, links, videos, likes, etc,)

Engagement Rate – Once you divide the number of engagements by the number of impressions for a certain tweet, you get the engagement rate.

Reach Percentage – It's calculated by dividing the number of tweet impressions by the total number of followers, and it shows how many followers saw the selected tweet.

Other great tools that Twitter Analytics offer are **'Audiences'** – where you can gather intel on your audience (location, gender, interests, etc.) and **'Ad Campaign Dashboard'** – where you will gain access to the performance of your active promotions.

Advertising on Twitter

If you want to keep your Tweets from getting lost in the whirlpool of active content, then giving them a little boost to make sure that they will be seen by your audience, seems like the smart thing to do.

Twitter ads can help you get the message to the right customers.

Type of Twitter Ads

There are a couple of ways in which you can promote on Twitter:

Promoted Tweets

These are tweets that you pay to make sure that people who are not already following you Twitter will see. Just like with regular tweets, the promoted tweets can also be liked, retweeted, shared, etc. The only difference between them and the regular tweets is in the **'Promoted'** sign next to them.

Promoted Accounts

Promoted accounts do not promote your Tweets but your Twitter profile. They help your account get discovered more and bring you more followers, by promoting your Tweeter profile to people who may be interested in your brand, but are not already following you.

Promoted Trends

Trends are those subjects on Twitter that people talk about the most. Promoted trends is an option that allows you to promote your own #hashtag at the top of the list of the most popular trends. So,

142

when Twitter users search for a specific trend, they will see a list of organic results, with your hashtag at the top. This will gain you more organic exposure and enhance your list of followers.

Automated Ads

Although customized Twitter ads are a better way to reach your specific business goal, there is another option for those that are unsure of how much they want to spend, have a limited time, or lack the strong team. That option is called *Twitter Promoted Mode*.

Twitter Promoted Mode are automated ads that you pay a flat fee for. With a fixed price of $99 (plus tax) per month, you can have your first 10 tweets (of the day) promoted to your target audience, automatically.

According to Twitter, you can expect to reach about 30,000 people with this option. Also, this will most likely get you approximately 30 new followers each month.

Creating Your Ad Campaign

Creating a Twitter ads campaign is a very straight forward process. Just follow the steps below and your Tweets are ready to be promoted.

#1: The Ads Account

If it is your first time using Twitter for advertising, you will need to have an account. Visit https://ads.twitter.com/login to get started.

#2: The Objective

Your ad campaign must be based on a specific objective for your business, meaning that this is the step where you decide what it is that you want to achieve with your Twitter ads. Whether it is to reach more followers, build your brand's awareness, increase the engagement rate or another reason, choose your objective wisely and click **'Next'** to continue.

#3: The Ad Group and Bidding

At this point, you choose your ad-group, which is a cub0category of your campaign. At this point, it is recommended to stick to a single ad-group, but as you become more comfortable with Twitter advertising, you can split it into a couple sub-groups to target different audiences or experiment with budgets and timing.

Here, you will also have to choose your budget, or how much you want to pay for every interaction (video view, engagement, etc.)

When you're all set, click **'Next'** for the next step.

#4: The Creative and Ad Placement

Select the tweet you want to promote from a list of old tweets, or simply create a new one here. Then, choose the ad placement:

- Users' timelines

- Profiles and Tweet detail pages

- Search results

Again, click **'Next'**.

#5: The Target Audience

Here, you need to go through several targeting options to select your preferred audience. You will have to select location, gender, age, language, technology, etc. in order to define the type of audience you want to promote your Tweets too. Also, you have the option to upload your own list of target audience (such as your email list), or you can also choose to target users that are similar to the audience who is already following you.

#6: The Launch

When you are all done, just click on **'Launch Campaign'** to start your campaign and launch your ads. And that's it.

LinkedIn

LinkedIn is the largest and most popular professional network with over 562 million users from all over the world. If you want to build your connections and expand your network, then being active on LinkedIn is an absolute must for your business. It is, after all, the top social network for lead generation.

Being a platform that connects companies and professionals, LinkedIn, most certainly, requires a unique marketing strategy. Here, the rule is the word of mouth. It is not about who you know, but about who can connect with through the people you know. But promoting your brand via your outdated personal page will not turn out to be a successful marketing plan. Read on to see how to create (and implement) your killer marketing strategy that will raise you to the top on LinkedIn.

Setting Up Your LinkedIn Company Page

To promote your brand on LinkedIn, you need a full-blown company page. The company page is a professional way to let LinkedIn users learn about your brand, your products, your company, as well as job opportunities that your company offers.

Although the company pages were primarily used as HR landing pages, now, this platform offers a great opportunity for increasing brand awareness and promoting your services to potential customers.

In order to set up a company page, you need an active LinkedIn personal profile first. Assuming that you have one, simply follow the next steps to create the page for your company.

Step #1: Add Your Company

Go to https://business.linkedin.com/marketing-solutions/linkedin-pages and click on **'Create Your Page'**. Enter the name of your company and come up with a URL that will help people find your page. Note that you cannot change the URL later, so make sure to choose wisely. Then, check the checkbox to verify that you are an official representative of the company and click on **'Create Page'**.

The shell is automatically created. To start building your page, just click on the **'Get Started'** button.

Step #2: Add Your Image

Upload your logo (300 x 300 pixels recommended) as your profile picture, and add a cover image (preferably 1536 x 768 px) to offer a glimpse of what your company is about. Keep in mind that companies with logos have more traffic, so do not be tempted to skip this step.

Step #3: Create Your Description

LinkedIn allows you to use 2,000 characters for your description, but be aware that it is the first 156 words that appear in your company page's preview that is displayed on Google, so make sure to write an outstanding beginning.

You have the option to add 20 specialties. Think of them as keywords ad they can help people discover your company on LinkedIn, so make sure to represents the strength and expertise of your business here.

Step #4: Your Company's Details

Here, you will enter the location of your company, your website's URL, your industry, size and type of your company, as well as other important details that describe your business.

Step #5: Publish the Page

To go live, click on **'Publish'**. Before you continue, it is recommended to check what the company page looks like when other users click on it. To check it out, click on **'Member View'**. If you are not satisfied the look of your page, go to **'Manage Page'** and make some changes.

Step #6: Page Administrators

If you are not planning to run your LinkedIn company page alone, then you will have to choose the people that can administer the page.

To add more employees, click on the **'Me'** button found at the top of your page. Then, go to **'Manage'**, choose your Company Page. There, choose **'Admin Tools'** → **'Page Admins'**. Then, enter the name of the people you want to give access to the page.

Note: You have to already be connected to these people on LinkedIn in order to select them as administrators.

The Perfect Strategy

Simply creating a company page doesn't mean that the right connections will come your way. Just like with any other platform, you need to have a good marketing strategy for LinkedIn as well. Here is what you can do in order to enhance your chance for success:

Create a Showcase Page

Showcase pages are the perfect way to showcase a specific part of your company that you are most proud of. This is a great opportunity to put the spotlight on your best product and attract potential customers.

The showcase pages work as some sort of subdomains for your company page, and having one can really make a difference as LinkedIn users can also follow them separately if they are specifically interested in a particular product or service. You can have up to showcase pages.

To create one, click on the **'Me'** button, and under **'Manage'**, select your Company Page. Then, go to **'Admin Tools'** ➔ **'Create a Showcase Page'**.

Have Your Employees Connected

Your biggest advocates on LinkedIn are your employees. Having them as followers means that you have access to their networks and connections, which can significantly expand your reach and bring more traffic to your Company Page. Encourage your employees to be linked with your Company Page to increase brand awareness.

Keep Followers Informed

The best way to boost your audience is to keep the one you have satisfied. Make sure to regularly publish valuable content such as articles, blog posts, or other updated on your company. Also, if you can think of an external article that can be valuable to your followers, do not hesitate to publish it as well.

Choose LinkedIn Groups

LinkedIn Groups offer a great way for you to connect with people from your field that are outside of your immediate circle. Being active in a LinkedIn Group and engaging in discussions can drive more traffic to your Page.

Want to find a Group that will match your goal? You can check out some LinkedIn suggestions with the **'Group Discover'** option, or simply use the search bar if you know what you are looking for.

Go Global

If you have customers in some countries where English is not the official language, then you might want to consider adding a description of your company written in other languages. Don't worry, you don't have to hire a translator for that purpose. LinkedIn offers multi-language tools that can take care of this for you.

Publish at the Right Times

Just like the strategies for your other platforms, your LinkedIn publishing must also be planned for. LinkedIn research says that the best time for content publishing on LinkedIn is in the morning and after business hours. This is when people are the most engaged, so you might want to take advantage of this information and schedule your post for then.

Advertising on LinkedIn

If you want to target your message to other professionals, whether CEOs or influencers, then advertising on LinkedIn is definitely something you should take advantage of. Once you determine *what* you want to advertise and *who* is your target audience, then you can proceed with the next steps.

Step #1: Your 'Campaign Manager' Account

First of all, to begin, you have to have a **'Campaign Manager'** account, which you can take care of here https://www.linkedin.com/ad-beta/login. This is a tool that helps you manage and optimize your ads in the most convenient way possible. Plus, this tool offers some beneficial tools that will display the performance of your ads, so that's an added bonus.

Step #2: Choose the Type of Your Ad

Next, you have to select the type of ad you want to promote. There are three options available:

1. Sponsored Content

2. Text Ads

3. Sponsored InMail

You can also create your campaign with all of the three formats to ensure the maximum possible reach.

Once you select the type of ad, enter the name of your campaign, choose the language of your target audience, and choose the call-to-action option, which is available only for the Sponsored-Content ads.

Step #3: Create the Ad

The best thing about the Campaign Manager is that it walks you through the steps of creation, offering you tips and help along the way. Follow the steps choosing the options that match your goal the most.

Step #4: Target the Ad

At this point, make sure that your ad will be targeted to the right people. You need to specify some criteria such as location, school names, company names, degree, job title, gender, age, years of experience, skills, etc. Make sure to save your criteria, so that you can speed things up the next time you wish to advertise on LinkedIn.

Step #5: Set the Budget and Schedule

There are three ways in which you can pay for the ads:

1. Cost Per Click (CPC)

2. Cost Per Impression (CPM) – for the messages in a member's view

3. Cost Per Send – for the Sponsored InMail ads (here, you pay only for those messages that are received)

For the CPM and CPS option, you are allowed to set a maximum daily budget you are willing to spend, and a bid price.

After that, simply schedule the start and end date and time for the ad, and you're done.

Is Your Marketing Strategy Working?

If you are pulling your metrics from another social media platform, then you are probably missing out on the real picture of your LinkedIn performance. The best way to check if your marketing strategy is working, is by checking out the built-in analytics tool on LinkedIn.

Go to the toolbar fount at the top of your page and click on the **'Analytics'** button. You will see that there are three available options:

Visitors - This is where data on the people who visit your page is stored. Here you can see the general overview of page view, the traffic metrics, you can isolate data from a specific time and date, see data from different pages on your profile, as well as see detailed information of the members who view your page (job function, location, industry, etc.)

Updates – Here you can find data about the content you share. These engagement metrics include the impressions, clicks, shares, likes, clicks, etc.

Followers – In the 'Followers' category, you can check out your list of followers in more detail.

Pinterest

Pinterest is that interesting platform where people plan their kids' unrealistic birthday parties. It is your go-to place when you are in need of inspiration, whether it is for remodeling your living room, getting a new haircut, or buying a pair of sneakers. But if you think that just because Pinterest is so much different than Facebook and Instagram, it is not worth the investment of time, money, and effort, for the purpose of promoting your brand, you cannot be more wrong.

It is the fact that people go there for inspiration that makes Pinterest a great platform for marketing your business. When your potential customers are searching for inspiration and solution, your products or services can be the thing that can solve their problems. And as Pinterest's motto suggests, this platform is perfect for reaching to your customers while they are making a decision.

Using Pinterest for Business

If you have a personal Pinterest account, you are probably familiar with their boards and pins. *Pins* are the images or videos that people save to their Pinterest account, while *boards* are the collections where pins are stores and organized (you'd want to keep the inspirations for your kid's birthday party in a different board than the one with your stew recipes).

But even though you may consider yourself to be a Pinterest guru, please, do not skip this chapter as business Pinterest is used differently.

Creating Your Business Pinterest Account

To market your business on Pinterest, you will need a business Pinterest account. This account is different as the one for personal use, as it offers the opportunity to advertise your content, as well as to track your metrics with Pinterest analytics.

To open a Pinterest business account, go to https://www.pinterest.com/business/create/, enter your email address and password, and click on **'Create Account'**. You will be asked to enter the name of your business, your website, as well as to choose the category that your business falls into.

Once you create your business account, you will see your feed page. This is only what you see. Your customers will only see your profile, which you can access by clicking on the red tack found in the upper right corner.

Completing Your Profile

Your profile may be created, but in order to be appealing to your followers, you will need to put in some work. First, you will need to have a profile picture uploaded. Click on **'Settings'** under your profile icon at the top right corner, scroll down, and upload your desired profile picture. Again, choose something that represents your business.

In the **'About'** section, make sure to add relevant information, use important keywords, and present your business in the best light possible. Add the location of your company and your website's URL. Once you're all set, click on **'Save Settings'**.

Confirming Your Website

This is probably the most important step when it comes to Pinterest marketing, as confirming your website throws a lot of benefits your way. Having a confirmed website will help you pinpoint what customers pin from your website, and will also add your logo next to each of the pins made from your website. And most importantly, having a confirmed website will increase you're the ranking of your Pins in search results.

To confirm your website, go to **'Settings'** and click on **'Confirm Website'** from the profile section.

Then, copy the text and paste it into the HTML of the index page of your website. Hit **'Finish'**.

Your Pinterest Boards

Now that your business account is ready, it is time for you to create your Pinterest boards so your customers will have a reason to follow you. Keep in mind that your customers don't need to follow your entire account. Once you create your boards, they can choose to follow one or multiple boards.

To start creating your boards, go to your Pinterest profile:

1. Click on the **'Boards'** tab, then hit the red '+' sign in order to create a new board.

2. Enter the desired name for the board. Make sure to use compelling and clear name for your board, and do not forget the keywords. Try to keep the name below 20 characters; otherwise it will get cut off in the search results.

3. To enter more details to your board, go back to the **'Boards'** tab, and click on the pencil icon.

4. Below the name, you will see that you need to enter a description. Describe what your board is about, keep in mind the keywords, and try to be as to-the-point as possible. Then, choose the category of your board.

5. If you are ready to start pinning, you can go right ahead, but if you are still unsure, know that you have the option to keep the board secret until you are ready to make it visible. That way, you can save your pins but your followers will not see them until you turn off the **'Secret'** option.

The Pinning

After creating your boards, the next step is to add some pins to them. The most convenient way to do so is to have a Pinterest browser button installed, which you can find here https://about.pinterest.com/en/browser-button. With the help of that button, you can Pin things with a few clicks:

1. After installing your Pinterest browser button, click on the Pinterest icon from your toolbar.

2. There, you will see a list of available options, choose your preferred image, then click **'Save'**.

3. Add your description.

4. Select the board that you wish to save the Pin to.

If you're using the mobile Pinterest app, things will be even simpler.

To choose the cover pin for your board, go to the **'Boards'** tab, and click on the pencil icon. Click on **'Cover'** → **'Change'** and then select your desired Pin.

Your Pinterest Strategy

Just like with other social media platforms, you also need to have a few tricks up your sleeve when it comes to marketing your brand on Pinterest. Here are some simple tips that will make your Pins' ranking skyrocket and get you more followers.

Create a User-Generated Board

The best way about Pinterest marketing is that you can let your followers contribute to your boards by adding their own pins there. This is a great opportunity for you to get in touch with your audience as well as to keep them engaged and interested in your products or services. Select a few of your top followers and dedicate a Pinboard to them. Ask them to pin images that display what they like and appreciate the most about your products and services. For instance, if you are offering a huge sale, your customers may Pin images of a fancy dinner that they paid with the saved money from the discount. This is a very unique way to showcase customer testimonials.

Pin Consistently and at the Right Time

Pinning once a day is optimal for the promotion of your brand on Pinterest. Pinterest says that its peak times are the evenings and the weekends, so you might want to take advantage of that. Pin once a day, in the evening, and consider to pin twice on Saturday or Sunday, when people are most active.

But Pinterest says that the key does not lie in the number of times you pin per day, but in the consistency. For instance, if you have 12 images to be pinned this week, then it is recommended to pin twice a day (two days only once), rather than pinning once a day and leaving the remaining 7 pins for the weekend.

Focus on the Visuals

Pinterest is a visual platform, which means that creating images of high-quality is not an option, but a must. If you do not have the skill or the right to tools to create your own, you may want to consider hiring someone for the part, or even purchasing some stock images to pin.

Also, try to showcase your product or service the best way possible. For instance, instead of pinning a close-up of your sunglasses, why not upload an image of a model on the beach, wearing your sunglasses. Pinterest says that those Pins that display people using a product are 67% more likely to drive sales.

Go for Rich Pins

Rich Pins are those Pins that contain additional info (metadata pulled from your website) about what your followers will find when they click on your Pins. For instance, Rich Pins for recipes include the ingredient list and also the button **'Make It'**, which is a great call-to-action. These Pins are also great for articles, products, apps, and in other words, almost anything that Pinners are looking to find.

Advertising on Pinterest

Similarly to the previously-explained advertising campaigns, promoting your brand on Pinterest also require a step-by-step process to go through. Here is how you can easily create a Pinterest ad campaign:

Step #1: Install the Pinterest Tag

Pinterest Tag is a tool that shows you what actions people take on your website after your Pins re-direct them there. This super-important tool will show you the sign-ups, checkouts, and searches that your followers make there, which will give you a clear insight of just how well your ads are performing. You can install the Pinterest tag here https://business.pinterest.com/en/pinterest-tag.

Step #2: Choose Your Objective

When you go to https://ads.pinterest.com/, the first think you will need to do is to select the objective from your ad. Here, there are only 4 available objectives:

1. Boost the Brand Awareness

2. Get Traffic to Your Site

3. Increase the Installs for Your App

4. Build an Awareness for Your Brand with Video Views

Step #3: Set the Budget

Here, you will be prompted to enter the name of your campaign, as well as to set the daily and lifetime budget.

Step #4: Create an Ad Group

Add groups are there to help you reach multiple goals for a limited budget, and within one ad campaign. It is recommended to launch 2-4 pins per an ad group.

Step #5: Choose the Target Audience

Go through the parameters for audience targeting and enter the desired preferences. Your target audience can be set based on the: gender, age, location, language, and devices.

Step #6: Choose the Ad Placement

At this point, you need to choose where your ad will be placed. If you have the means for it, choose the recommended, ALL placement. If not, you can either choose *Browse* (these placements end up in the user's home feed as related pins) or *Search* (these placements are recommended for keyword targeting).

Step #7: Add Keywords and Interests

To further optimize your targeting, you should take advantage of interests and keywords. This feature will ensure that your ads are targeted to the relevant searches. You have over 3400 interests to choose from, so you can rest assured that you will find the best ones for your business. For best results, use twenty-five keywords. You can also use negative keywords if there is something you want to exclude from the search.

Step #8: Set the Budget and Schedule

Enter the start and end date of your campaign and select how much you are willing to spend, on daily and lifetime basis. Make sure to make no mistake here as this option cannot be edited and changed later on.

Step #9: Optimization and Delivery

Here, set the maximum bid for your Pinterest ad. The minimum bid is $2.

Step #10: Determine the Pacing

You have Standard Pacing and Accelerated Pacing to choose from. The standard option is what aligns the bids and spending with the duration of the campaign, while the accelerated pacing enables fast delivery of the budget, and is recommended for those campaigns that have higher impact. To keep it simple, the standard pacing will not spend over your set limit, while the accelerated option can spend your limit way before the end date of your campaign.

Step #11: Select the Pins

Click on **'Pick a Pin'** to select the Pins you wish to add to your ad group. As mentioned earlier, each of your ad group should have between 2 to 4 Pins. In order for your Pins to be able to be added to your ad group they have to be saved on your profile and not on a secret board, have URLs (not shortened), and they shouldn't feature some third-party videos or GIFs.

Pinterest Analytics

Pinterest Analytics, unlike the Pinterest Tag, provides valuable information about which of your Pins perform best on the platform, not your website. This helpful tool offers metrics that allow you to keep a track of the performance of the Pins in order to gain insight of what should be changed and improved on your business Pinterest profile, in order to drive traffic and get more followers.

Besides the metrics, here you can also see the boards that people saved your Pins to, which can help you determine what people associate your business with and what they think about your brand and the products and services that you are offering.

To access your Pinterest Analytics, go to your profile and click on the **'Analytics'** tab found in the upper left corner.

The best metrics to track with Pinterest Analytics are:

Impressions – They measure the reach of your content and represent the number of Pins that appear in the search results, home feed, and category feeds.

Closeups – This represents the number of time that people tap on your Pin in order to have a better look at it.

Clicks – The number of re-directs from your Pins to your website.

Repins – This shows the number of time Pinterest users saved your Pin to their boards.

Top Pins – Here are displayed the pins that have been performing the best in the last month.

Top Boards – Your most popular boards in the last 30 days.

All-Time Stats – This is a long-view data great for determining what has worked for your Pinterest profile and what, in order to optimize your account.

Audience Affinities – Affinities show you the type of content that your audience is most engaged with.

Conclusion

Now that you've learned all about social media marketing, the next step is to create your accounts and get started with promoting your brand online.

But remember, this is not your magic bullet. A good marketing strategy can only be successful if you invest time, effort, and most importantly if you engage with your audience

The social media marketing climate may seem unstable, but the forecast is definitely bright for brands who listen, learn, and want to improve and optimize for successful results.

www.ingramcontent.com/pod-product-compliance
Lightning Source LLC
Chambersburg PA
CBHW072255210326
41458CB00074B/1739